Hans Feibusch
The Heat of Vision

I know that a small photograph of a few details means little; that perhaps only the real thing in its full size, colour and surface quality, and in its surroundings, can bring the deep impact that will go on vibrating through one's life. It is this emotion, this heat of vision, that are wanted; we live in times of such picturesqueness, greatness and tragedy as any this old continent of ours has witnessed; our experience and insight have deepened under the almost apocalyptic uncertainty in which everything takes on a new, queer significance. The rough material out of which great art can be created is under our hands and, what is more important, we have been shaken up sufficiently to see its symbolical aspect. The work of our best artists, Paul Nash, Henry Moore, Graham Sutherland, John Piper, Edward Bawden, has all the terrible and moving quality of our time ... But whatever we choose or are given as subject, the imprint of our age must be on what we paint; the strange and furious glow has been shining on us too long not to have penetrated into every crevice of our world.

Hans Feibusch, *Mural Painting*, 1946, p.65

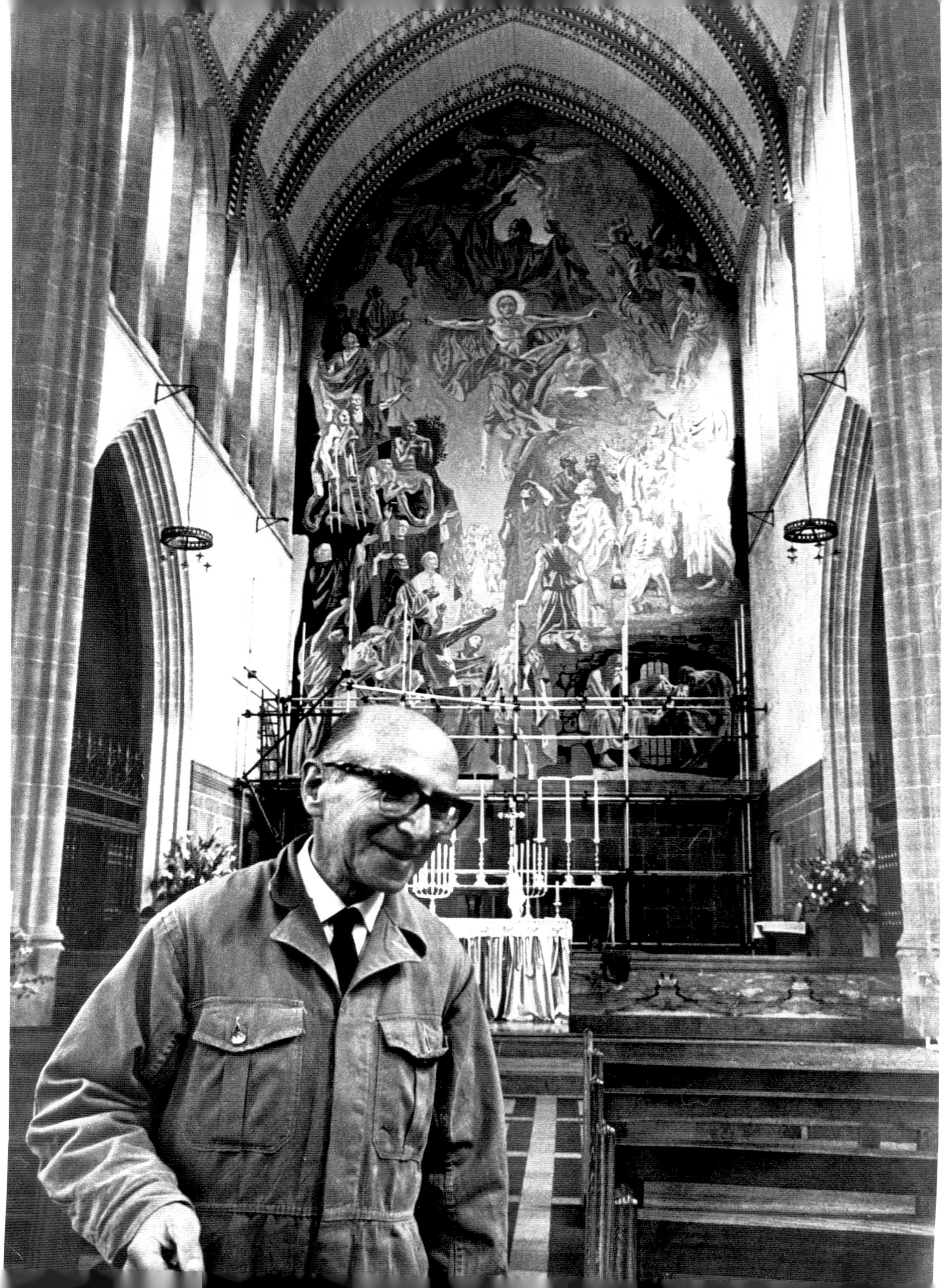

Edited by David Coke

Hans Feibusch

The Heat of Vision

Lund Humphries Publishers, London
in association with
Pallant House Gallery Trust, Chichester

First published in 1995 by
Lund Humphries Publishers Ltd
Park House
1 Russell Gardens
London NW11 9NN
in association with
Pallant House Gallery Trust, Chichester
Reg. Charity No. 293093

on the occasion of the touring exhibition
HANS FEIBUSCH: THE HEAT OF VISION
A Retrospective Exhibition of Works from 1930 to 1995

Pallant House Gallery, Chichester
5 September – 21 October 1995

Ben Uri Art Gallery, London
6 November – 10 December 1995

Northampton Museum and Art Gallery
20 January – 25 February 1996

Towner Art Gallery, Eastbourne
16 March – 28 April 1996

Newport Museum and Art Gallery
18 May – 29 June 1996

British Library Cataloguing in Publication Data
A catalogue record for this book is available from the British Library

ISBN 0 85331 670 8

PALLANT HOUSE

Pallant House, an early-eighteenth-century townhouse in the centre of Chichester, was opened to the public in 1982, following the offer of Dr Walter Hussey, Dean of Chichester Cathedral from 1955 until 1977, to bequeath his fine art collection to the city if it could be displayed at Pallant House (then local authority offices). Hussey, one of the great patrons of church art this century, who had been invited to Chichester by Bishop Bell, was an old friend of Feibusch. He was the first churchman to respond to Feibusch's 'call to arms' in his book *Mural Painting* of 1946 'to let churches be decorated by such men as Georges Rouault or Graham Sutherland, in whom there is fire … the voice of the Church should be heard loud over the thunderstorm; and the artist should be her mouthpiece, as of old'.

After the acceptance by the Chichester District Council of Dean Hussey's offer, and the restoration of Pallant House itself, Hussey's collection, consisting largely of modern British works by such artists as Henry Moore, Graham Sutherland, John Piper, Ceri Richards, Paul Nash, Ben Nicholson and Ivon Hitchens, was later joined by a second bequest, a compatible collection containing works by many of the same artists as well as a handful of foreign artists – Gino Severini, Paul Klee, André Derain, Jean-Paul Riopelle and others. The nucleus of these two bequests now forms the basis for additional acquisitions, and for an annual programme of loan exhibitions. Put Pallant House together with the modern works in the Cathedral by John Piper, Graham Sutherland and Marc Chagall, and the teaching collection at the Chichester Institute including works by artists such as Stanley Spencer, Alfred Wallis, Graham Sutherland, Peter Lanyon, Patrick Heron, Willi Soukop and Lucie Rie, and Chichester can be seen to be a major centre for the study and enjoyment of modern British art.

Exhibition generously supported by
the Embassy of the Federal Republic of Germany

FRONTISPIECE
Hans Feibusch at work on *The Trinity in Glory*
at Saint Alban the Martyr, Holborn, London, 1965

Typeset in Ehrhardt
Designed by Alan Bartram
Photography of paintings by Roy Fox
Made and printed in Great Britain by BAS Printers Limited, Over Wallop, Hampshire

Contents

Preface

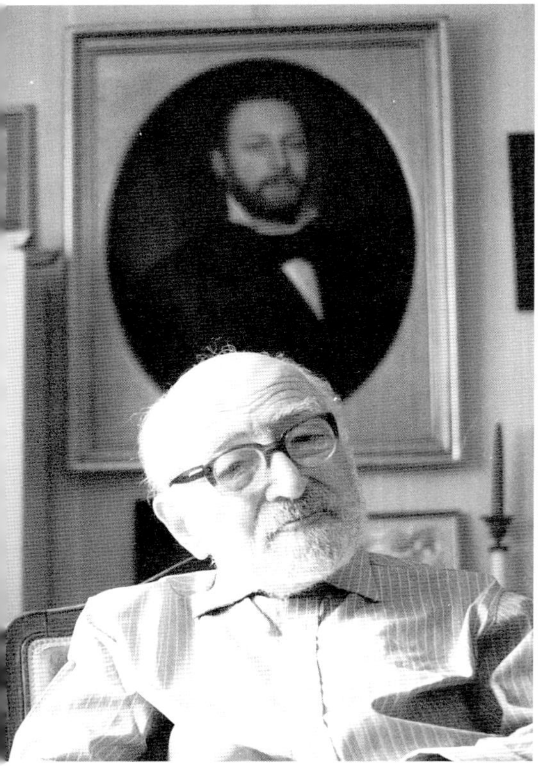

Hans Feibusch seated below a portrait of his grandfather, 1994. Photograph by Gaynor Williams

Hans Feibusch is the artist of the glowing palette. Born in 1898 and still working today, his subjects are figurative and are drawn from three main themes: the mythological world of gods and heroes, the fertile ground of the Bible, and the natural world around us.

Exiled from Germany in 1933 after his work had been reviled, banned and eventually destroyed by the Nazis, Feibusch made a major artistic contribution to the reconstruction of post-war Britain through his extraordinary series of mural paintings. Much of his early work in this field came to him through Thomas F. Ford, an architect who restored many bombed churches after the war. Ford worked in the practice of E. Maxwell Fry, who was a close friend of Feibusch over many years, and who also introduced him, and his work, to many people. (Coincidentally, Fry was also a close friend of Charles Kearley, one of Pallant House's principal benefactors.)

But Feibusch's greatest patron was George Bell, Bishop of Chichester, who over the years commissioned several major murals from Feibusch, one of which is in Chichester Cathedral (M9, p.24), and another in the Bishop's private chapel adjacent to the Bishop's Palace (M13, p.25). Bishop Bell was strongly in favour of the church using living artists, and soon after the war he convened a weekend meeting to re-awaken the relationship between contemporary artists and the church. Feibusch was at this meeting, as were John Piper, Henry Moore, T. S. Eliot, Dorothy L. Sayers, Edward Maufe, Charles Wheeler and Father Martin D'Arcy.

From the See of Chichester, Feibusch's name as a muralist spread throughout the country; but he also produced easel paintings, gouaches, drawings, lithographs and sculpture. It is hard to understand why the diversity and richness of the work of this prodigious artist has never before been adequately shown. This exhibition gives a unique chance to study and enjoy the work of a contemporary figurative artist whose career spans more than six decades of one of the most vibrantly creative periods in the history of British art.

Included in the exhibition are almost ninety examples of the best of the artist's work in all media, from the past sixty-five years of his long career. One surprise amongst the main body of work is a beautifully observed and finely drawn series of pencil studies of animals at London Zoo.

Any retrospective exhibition is bound to be a subjective view of the artist's work. The organisers of *The Heat of Vision* certainly plead guilty to allowing personal taste to influence their choice, but have endeavoured to show a selection of the most important of Hans Feibusch's work, that work which best reflects his own strongly held views, and which is most specifically 'Feibusch-esque', as far as that is quantifiable. Some areas of the artist's work are, of necessity, absent, having been lost or destroyed during the war. We have included no still-lifes, and only a small proportion of the artist's total output of landscape paintings – although Feibusch produced large numbers of pictures in both these areas, on the whole they do not represent any significant advance in the development of his art.

The exhibition has been made possible by the generous help of a number of people. It would have been impossible without the unstinting assistance of Paul Werth, the son of Feibusch's step-daughter. It is unlikely that he knew how much he was taking on when he first agreed to offer his active participation. Gaynor Williams, Honorary Education Officer of Art History at Pallant House, has given many hours of time to help the Curator in selecting the exhibition, and to undertake much of the preliminary photography and research. Grateful thanks are also due to the contributors to the catalogue – Hans Tisdall, Jutta Vinzent and Bishop Walker; to Kathrine Talbot for her translation of German texts; to Dr John Gage, Professor of Art History at Cambridge University, for putting us in touch with Jutta Vinzent; and to Mrs S. M. Newton for her kind permission to allow us to reproduce Eric Newton's essay of 1949 on the mural paintings of Hans Feibusch.

Finally, I would like to express my own very deep gratitude to Hans Feibusch himself for waiting around long enough for me to realise that here was an artist, with close associations with Chichester, who was a natural subject for a Pallant House exhibition; an artist who deserved a very much wider public, and who had, inexplicably, never been accorded a retrospective exhibition in his adopted country, despite many other honours, both here and in Germany.

Feibusch's citation for the Honorary Doctorate of Letters awarded to him by the Archbishop of Canterbury at Lambeth in 1985 reads: 'In recognition of his services in promoting the association of artists and the Church through his work as a painter, sculptor and writer.' This exhibition honours his creative contribution to the development of twentieth-century British art, a contribution that will only become obvious in time and after very much more public exposure of his work.

DAVID COKE
Curator of Pallant House Gallery since 1981.

Chronology

1898
Born 15 August, the son of Dr Carl Feibusch and Marianne Ickelheimer, in Frankfurt-am-Main.

1916
From November 1916 until June 1918 served in the German army. Posted to the Russian Front.

1918
After two terms of medicine, he began his formal study of painting in Munich in the studio of Polish artist Stanislas Stückgold.

1920
Studied in Berlin under Karl Hofer. Completed studies as a 'Meisterschüler' (Master Student).

1921–3
Studied in Italy: Florence, Rome, Perugia, Pisa and Venice.

1923–4
Studied in Paris in the studios of Othon Friesz and André Lhote. Exhibited at the *Salon d'Automne* and the *Paris Indépendants*.

1925
Returned to Frankfurt. Member of the Frankfurt Artists' Association until 1933. Group exhibitions in Frankfurt, Berlin and Düsseldorf. Took part in annual exhibitions of the Prussian Academy of Arts and of the Berlin Secession until 1932.

1929
23 January: Death of his brother.
15 February: Death of his father.

1930
December: Awarded the German Grand State Prize for Painters by the Prussian Academy of Arts in Berlin for the painting *The Fishmonger*.

1933
May: Germans refused to renew his passport.
September: Emigrated to England, settled in London.

1934
First one-man exhibition at the Lefevre Gallery, London.

1935
Married Sidonie Gestetner.
Became a member of the London Group.

1936
One-man exhibition at the Lefevre Gallery.

1937
His work *Zwei schwebende Figuren* (*Two Floating Figures*) of 1932 was shown in the 'Degenerate Art' exhibition in Munich. As a Jew, his work was banned and destroyed by the Nazis.

1938
Granted British citizenship.
Emigration of his mother to London.
First public commission: *Footwashing* in the Methodist Chapel, Colliers Wood, London. The chapel has since been demolished and the painting (on panel) lost.
Exhibited *Death of Narcissus* (1938) in the *Exhibition of Twentieth-Century German Art* in London.
One-man exhibition at the Lefevre Gallery.

1939
First commission from Dr George Bell, Bishop of Chichester, to paint a mural for one of the churches in his diocese, St Wilfrid's, Brighton: *The Nativity*.

1942
One-man exhibition at the Lefevre Gallery: *Religious and Other Paintings by Hans Feibusch*.

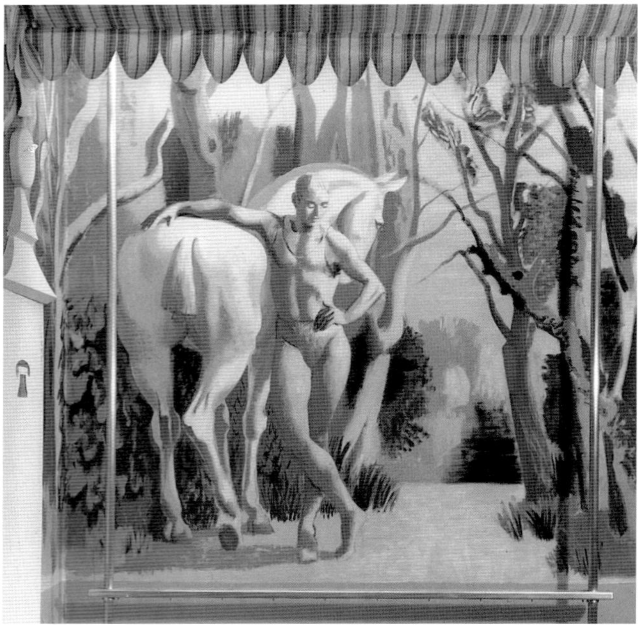

Circus Folk (detail) 1948
These temporary murals (M5) were painted for the tea pavilion of the *Britain Can Make It* exhibition at the Victoria and Albert Museum. Photograph by Sydney W. Newbery

1944
First exhibited at the Royal Academy of Arts Summer Exhibition. (He exhibited on thirteen further occasions between 1944 and 1970, and again in 1985.)

1946
Publication of *Mural Painting*, a treatise on the history, theory and technique of the art.
Publication of *The Revelation of Saint John the Divine* with thirteen colour lithographs and endpapers by Feibusch.

1948
Decorated the tea pavilion at the Victoria and Albert Museum for the *Britain Can Make It* exhibition.

1950
Wrote the Foreword for the catalogue of the first exhibition of the Society of Mural Painters, as well as contributing an exhibit: *Pastoral*.

1951
Fifth one-man exhibition at the Lefevre Gallery, London.
Contributed *The Return of the Prodigal Son* (1950) to the *Sixty Paintings for '51* Arts Council exhibition. This mural panel was originally commissioned by George Bell for All Saints Church, Iden, where it still hangs today.

1960
Commissioned by the Newport Borough Council to paint a large mural cycle for the Central Hall, Newport Civic Centre.

1963
Death of Sidonie, his wife.

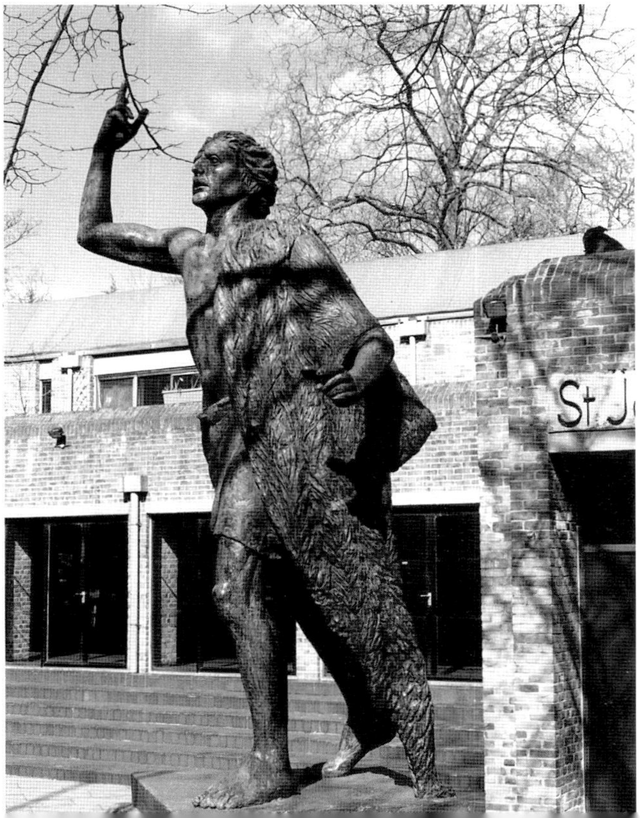

1967
Awarded the German Order of Merit, First Class.

1970
Because of failing eyesight he turned to sculpture, producing over the next ten years a number of portrait heads, as well as biblical and mythological figures, including, in 1973, a seven-foot figure of St John for St John's Wood Church, London. He returned to painting in the early 1980s after successful eye surgery restored his sight.

1978
Contributed a sketch for a *Resurrection* mural to the exhibition *Jewish Artists of Great Britain* at the Belgrave Gallery and Cartwright Hall, Bradford.
Hans Feibusch: An Eightieth Birthday Exhibition at The Orangery, Holland Park, London, organised by the Greater London Council.

1978–9
One-man exhibition at Galerie Michael Haas, Berlin: *Hans Feibusch*.

1985
Bronze figure of the *Risen Christ* for Saint Alban the Martyr, Holborn, London.
Awarded an Honorary Doctorate of Letters by the Archbishop of Canterbury at Lambeth Palace.
Exhibited *The Madonna of the Sunflowers* at the Royal Academy of Arts Summer Exhibition.

1986
One-man exhibition at the Historisches Museum, Frankfurt-am-Main: *Hans Feibusch: Ein Frankfurter Maler*.

1988
One-man exhibition at the Burstow Gallery, Brighton: *Hans Feibusch: Muralist, Painter, Sculptor*.

1989
Awarded the German Grand Cross of Merit.

1992
Formally left the Church of England after more than twenty years.

1993
3 November: A seminar given by Tom Devonshire Jones and Alan Powers on Hans Feibusch's life and work to celebrate his 95th birthday. Organised by the Twentieth Century Society and church of Saint Alban the Martyr, Holborn, London.

LEFT
St John 1973, outside St John's Wood Church, London NW8.
Cast resin. Photograph by David Coke

Exiled Artists: Their Impact on British Art in the 1930s and 1940s

Jutta Vinzent

When Hans Feibusch moved to Great Britain in 1933, he, together with thousands of people, was seeking refuge from the totalitarian Nazi regime.

Reasons for Emigrating

The Propaganda Ministry, established on 13 March 1933, was the embodiment of Nazi cultural policy. As its head Joseph Goebbels exerted pressure on German cultural life. All branches of culture – art, theatre, music, radio and film – came under his supervision. Everyone who produced, reproduced, spread, preserved, or sold cultural items had to become a member of the *Reichskulturkammer*, founded on 22 September 1933, which reserved the right to reject applicants. Unaffiliated artists were banned from their profession: in fact, excluded artists could no longer exhibit their work and were branded as 'degenerate'. Three main groups of artists were automatically rejected from the *Reichskulturkammer*, and forced to emigrate if they wished to continue working: Jewish artists; artists who were Communists or who belonged to the Social Democratic Party; and lastly, artists who were rejected purely because of the style of their works.

More than 210 German-speaking painters, sculptors, graphic artists and photographers emigrated to Great Britain between 1933 and 1945. While the specific reasons for their exodus are not always fully understood, the majority emigrated because they, their spouse, or their parents were Jewish. Hans Feibusch's parents were Jewish, and although they were not so religious as to give their son an orthodox Jewish upbringing, he was, neverthless, persecuted by the Nazis merely for belonging to the Jewish 'race'.[1]

The harassment of the Jews started immediately after Hitler's appointment as German Chancellor, and one incident in particular hastened Feibusch's decision to leave. A man in Nazi uniform appeared at a meeting of the *Frankfurter Künstlerbund*, a local organisation of artists to which Feibusch had belonged since 1925. The Nazi pointed to all the Jewish artists sitting around the table and told them that it would no longer be possible for them to exhibit their work.[2] Shocked by this event, Feibusch planned his emigration.

Most Jewish artists left Germany in 1933 and 1934 just after Hitler's appointment as German Chancellor, when the policy of displaying the so-called 'degenerate art' and of banning it from museums began, or just before the outbreak of the war, in 1938 and 1939. Most of the political fugitives, like Peter Peri and Theo Balden, belonged to the Communist party; a few, like Fred Uhlmann and Jan Tschichold, were adherents of socialist ideas. After the Nazis had become the state party and other parties had been prohibited (on 14 July 1933), these political opponents were designated enemies of the state, and had immediately to seek refuge.

It was the infamous 'Degenerate Art' exhibition in 1937 that represented the culmination of the Nazis' denigration of modern art. Artists such as Kurt Schwitters, Oskar Kokoschka and László Moholy-Nagy, who were persecuted purely for the style of their work, were included, as were Ludwig Meidner, Jankel Adler and John Heartfield. Several paintings by Feibusch's teacher Karl Hofer were displayed, along with one painting by Hans Feibusch. This picture, *Zwei schwebende Figuren* of 1932,[3] was displayed in a room designated solely for works by Jewish artists. These paintings were hung under the heading 'Revelation of the Jewish Racial Soul'.[4]

The Arrival of Hans Feibusch in London

Although Feibusch considered emigrating to Italy or France, his final decision to move to England was influenced by the fact that his wife-to-be Sidonie Gestetner, whom he had met in Germany, was British.

He emigrated to London in May 1933. He had been given a letter of recommendation from the head of the Staedelsches Kunstinstitut in Frankfurt, Georg Swarzenski, addressed to the Curator of the Tate Gallery in London,[5] but it was, nevertheless, not an easy beginning for Feibusch, as German art was still little known in England.[6] He eked out a living producing book illustrations and jacket designs, and posters for Shell and London Underground.

In the 1930s and 1940s the British avant-garde was dominated by abstract art, although a second important trend was Social Realism. These movements, at the same time contradictory and complementary, indicated a reaction to the prevailing insecurity and inhumanity in Europe, and corresponded exactly to two tendencies which Herbert Read discerned in modern art. In abstract art he perceived a 'search for formal harmony', while Social Realism represented a 'desire to express the chaos itself'.[7] Hans Feibusch did not fall into either of these two categories: he turned instead to religious subjects, exhibiting a search for spiritual guidance.

The persecution he experienced as a Jew made Feibusch more aware of his religion, as is evident in an untitled

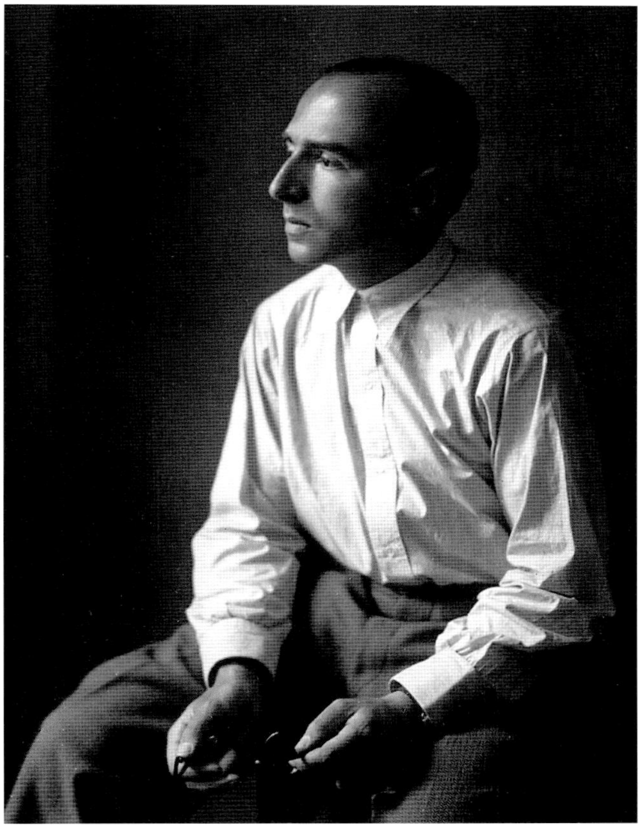

Studio portrait of Hans Feibusch *c.*1930

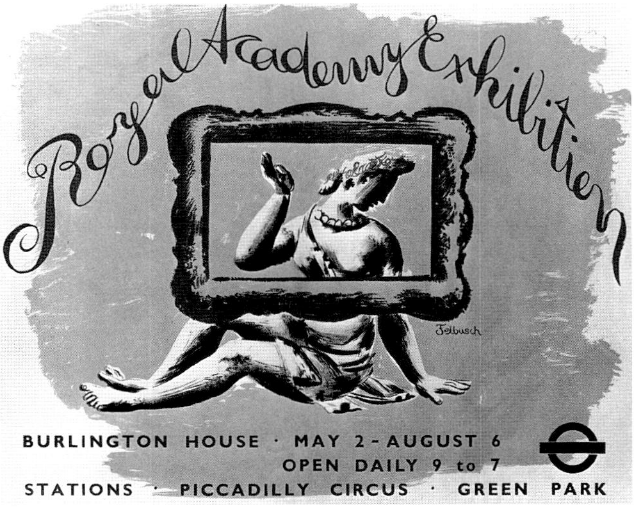

Poster designed by Hans Feibusch for London Underground, 1938. Courtesy of London Transport Museum

painting completed in the year of his emigration,[8] which depicts a man sitting on the floor, his arms held aloft in the gesture of prayer. In the background of the picture is the yellow star of David, which all German Jews were forced to wear on their clothes under the Nazi regime. Feibusch, however, did not turn to the Jewish religion, but rather to the belief that the chaos of life is only bearable with the faith of spiritual direction, irrespective of a specific religious community.

Although he did not start painting religious themes in mural paintings until he came to Britain, Feibusch was already artistically prepared to execute murals. After having finished his studies in Berlin with Karl Hofer, he had travelled to Italy and France, where he admired and studied Renaissance mural paintings. Furthermore, the artistic group he was a member of in Frankfurt in the 1920s and 1930s had been commissioned to paint a series of murals in the town. Never having formally studied mural painting, this opportunity inspired Feibusch to further explore the history and technique of this art. His first public commission in Britain, *Footwashing* (1938), was for the Methodist Chapel at Colliers Wood and so necessarily depicted a Christian theme.[9] This commission came to Feibusch via the architect E. Maxwell Fry, a fellow member of the London Group. Kenneth Clark saw a reproduction of this mural in *The Times*, and recommended Feibusch to George Bell, the Anglican Bishop of Chichester from 1929 to 1958. Bell was interested in bringing church and contemporary artists together, believing that the

> re-association of the Church and the arts was an effective protection against barbarism, whether the barbarism was Nazism, materialism or any other threat to civilization. He was concerned about the spiritual poverty he saw in contemporary society and he believed that the visual arts had an ability to teach about Christianity that few other disciplines had.[10]

Bell became Feibusch's greatest patron and was to commission many mural paintings, including those for Chichester Cathedral and Bell's private chapel next to the Bishop's Palace.

During the war Feibusch painted mainly in oil and gouache. These works were exhibited in a series of one-man shows at the Lefevre Gallery, London between 1934 and 1951, a gallery where other exiled artists also displayed their works.[11] Feibusch's reputation as a mural painter grew after the war through his contribution to the restoration of bomb-damaged churches. In total he produced around forty mural paintings, sited in Anglican churches in the Midlands and South of England, assisted in those days by Phyllis Bray, a painter in her own right, who had an excellent feeling for colour.

Feibusch's interest in, and experience of, the relationship between painting and architecture additionally led him to write *Mural Painting*, published in 1946:

We are on the outset of a new building era; tremendous tasks are to be undertaken, and we have, by lucky coincidence or providence, a new and vigorous architecture to tackle them. At the same time the interest in mural painting is reviving amongst architects, painters and the public; the hopes for a great art to rise up again are higher than they have been for the last 150 years; but there is also great danger that naive enthusiasm and lack of knowledge might cause speedy disillusionment.[12]

To help the reader overcome this lack of knowledge, Feibusch analyses the artistic achievements of muralists from past to present, surveying contemporary works such as Picasso's *Guernica*. He puts forward the idea that the mural painter should not 'tone himself down for the sake of the architecture'. Certainly, there are some governing rules and limits as in every other discipline but, 'Once the painter has understood the particular requirements he will be able to give his very best and express himself as completely as in an easel painting'.[13] Feibusch expresses the wish that:

We shall be spared, I hope, another outcrop of monumental banalities such as the last war brought us, and those immense, theatrical or pedestrian agglomerations of portraits or guns with which the museums of all countries were embarrassed. The war, altogether, can only be painted by those who were in the thick of it, and even they will have to let the overwhelming experience settle down for a number of years before they can begin to shape it. But whatever we choose or are given as subject, the imprint of our age must be on what we paint; the strange and furious glow has been shining on us too long not to have penetrated into every crevice of our world.[14]

The book ends with a technical section and some personal advice from the artist. Both the book and Feibusch's murals constituted a major artistic contribution to the reconstruction of post-war Britain.

The Impact of Refugee Artists on British Art

In the England of the 1930s and 1940s abstract art was dominated by Barbara Hepworth, Ben Nicholson and Henry Moore. They belonged to *Unit One*, a group of eleven artists founded in 1933 by Paul Nash. Living and working together in Hampstead, these artists had a common goal, although there was little stylistic unity in their work. The members of the group wanted to break with the traditional concept of art as the representation of nature. They did not deny nature, but as Nash put it 'art, we are inclined to feel, should control' it.[15] In 1934 the group held a touring exhibition and published their manifesto *Unit One*. However, while the show was still on tour, the group broke up. The members moved apart in two directions: Paul Nash towards Surrealism, while Ben Nicholson and Barbara Hepworth transferred to Constructivism. Henry Moore kept a foot in both camps.

Whereas British Surrealists looked to their counterparts in Paris, British abstract art was influenced by the exiled artists, in particular Naum Gabo. Hepworth and Nicholson's friendship with Naum Gabo was instrumental in motivating their experimentation with Constructivism. Gabo, the most influential exponent of Constructivism, was born in Russia, but received his artistic education in Munich and lived in Berlin from 1922 to 1932. In 1932 he went to Paris, where he met Hepworth and Nicholson who had gone there for a study visit. When Gabo arrived in Britain in 1935, they invited him to live with them in Hampstead.

One of the most important events for abstract art was the *Abstract and Concrete* exhibition shown at London, Cambridge, Oxford and Liverpool in 1936. Hepworth, Nicholson and Moore, together with other British artists, exhibited their works alongside exiled artists such as Naum Gabo and László Moholy-Nagy (who had arrived in May 1935, but only stayed in England until July 1937). The exhibited works reflected a desire for simplicity and clarity. It was during this show that Gabo really made contact with Nicholson and the architect Leslie Martin. A year later they published the English Constructivist manifesto *Circle*,[16] to which Gabo contributed the lead essay, his highly influential article 'The Constructive Idea in Art':

The basis of the constructive idea in art lies in an entirely new approach to the nature of art and its functions in life ... It has revealed a universal law that the elements of a visual art such as lines, colours, shapes, possess their own forces of expression independent of any association with the external aspects of the world ... Those elements ... are immediately and organically bound up with human emotions ... To find the means for the accomplishment of [his] task the artist need not search in the external world of nature; he is able to express his impulses in the language of those absolute forms which are in the substantial possession of his art.[17]

Gabo's article encouraged artists to make their art more abstract. For Hepworth, Constructivism reflected an absolute belief in human beings, in landscape and in the universal relationship of Constructive ideas. For a few years, Hepworth and Moore, like Gabo, explored the use of strings to convey 'transparent' planes in their sculptures. While Moore professed that he 'had been greatly intrigued by some of the mathematical models' in the Science Museum in London,[18] it is striking that he produced his first stringed figure in the very year that *Circle* was published.

One of the younger artists who also admired Naum Gabo was Peter Lanyon who was working with the Hampstead group, which had by that time moved to St Ives. He found Gabo's work exciting and after seeing a perspex construction by Gabo he commented: 'He was trying to define space, and space after all has no quality.'[19] Gabo's impact on abstract art persisted long after he left Britain for America in 1946, as is evident in the work of artists such as Victor Pasmore. Pasmore turned to abstraction in the late 1940s and some of his works, like *Relief Construction in White, Black and Maroon* of 1956-7, were based on Gabo's Constructivist ideas, and mark the flowering of a true Constructivist movement in Britain.

Curiously, the most representative German movement at

that time, Expressionism, did not really influence Britain in the 1930s and 1940s.[20] Although several exiled Expressionists fled to Great Britain, it seems that the English did not really appreciate the style. Oskar Kokoschka, the most famous Expressionist who emigrated to Great Britain, never had a one-man exhibition in England and no British gallery bought any of his work during his exile. Raymond Mortimer, although known for his liberal opinions and his lively and provocative style of writing, strongly criticised the *Exhibition of Twentieth-Century German Art* held in London in 1938: 'People who go to see the exhibition are only too likely to say: "If Hitler doesn't like these pictures, it's the best thing I've heard about Hitler." For the general impression made by the show on the ordinary public must be one of extraordinary ugliness.'[21]

Artists against Fascism

In the 1930s a number of artists' associations sprang up in protest at the Fascist tendencies they saw growing in Europe. In 1933 Cliff Rowe, Misha Black and others, all of whom belonged to the Communist party, founded the Artists' International Association (AIA). Their aim was to mobilise the 'international unity of artists against Imperialist War on the Soviet Union, Fascism and Colonial oppression'.[22] Initially, the members of the AIA were restricted to adherents of Social Realism. This changed, however, in the following years when the AIA affiliated with the English Group of Surrealists, the London Group and the New English Art Club. In 1936 the AIA numbered over 600 members, all united by the desire to fight against Fascism and war. Members did not necessarily belong to the Communist party nor were they all adherents of Communist ideas. Hans Feibusch, for example, who had belonged to the London Group since 1935, showed his works in the exhibitions of the AIA, although he had no wish actively to participate in politics.[23] Feibusch, along with other exiled artists such as Peter Peri and László Moholy-Nagy, and over 500 artists from England, France, Belgium, the Netherlands, Poland and USSR, participated in the *Artists Against Fascism & War* exhibition, which was held in London from 13 to 27 September 1935. Feibusch displayed his *Man with Outstretched Arms*. Exhibitions such as this were organised to help the few German-speaking immigrants who arrived in Britain before 1938. The fugitives were also offered membership of the AIA.

The most influential German art exhibition, the *Exhibition of Twentieth-Century German Art*, was held at the New Burlington Galleries in London from 7 July to 26 August 1938. Herbert Read was Chairman of the organising committee, and he received help from the Surrealist Roland Penrose, among others. In view of the prevailing Appeasement policy, the exhibition could probably not have been held without the help of such prominent English figures. In this show Feibusch exhibited his *Death of Narcissus* of 1938.

After the Munich Agreement on 30 September 1938 the situation for the immigrants who had fled to Prague deteriorated and Oskar Kokoschka, Theo Balden and others feared that they would be extradited to Germany. Roland Penrose received a request to rescue the members of the *Oskar-Kokoschka-Bund*, to which most of the émigré artists in Prague belonged. He organised a meeting to which he invited anti-Fascist artists and art critics, who belonged mainly to the AIA. They decided to found the Artists' Refugee Committee (ARC) to rescue the artists in Prague. Because of the British immigration requirements, the ARC had to find guarantors and hosts for the affected artists, and collect money to help them emigrate. The ARC raised £1600 through a petition which was signed by, amongst others, Henry Moore, Paul Nash, Vanessa Bell, Jacob Epstein, Roland Penrose (for the Surrealist Group), Richard Carline (for the London Group) and Stephen Bone (for the New English Art Club). Among the guarantors they secured was H. G. Wells, the president of the Pen Club, who enabled the artist John Heartfield to emigrate.

By 1938 almost all the German-speaking artists who would seek refuge in Britain, around 200 in total, had emigrated. It was in this year that Juergen Kuczynski, Johann Fladung, John Heartfield, Oskar Kokoschka and Alfred Kerr founded the Free German League of Culture (FGLC).

In the years that followed, the FGLC worked together with the ARC and AIA. The ARC was at that time campaigning for the release from British internment camps of the German-speaking immigrants who, deemed 'enemy aliens', were interned after the beginning of the war in 1939.

The FGLC also organised exhibitions with the AIA in London during the Second World War, such as *Works by Refugees and their English Friends* (19 June - 9 August 1941) and *Free German Artists* (June 1944). The FGLC disbanded in 1946 as many of its members, like John Heartfield, were closely connected with Communism, and left for East Germany after the end of the war. In 1946 the left wing of the AIA put forward the idea of a future for 'Britain between East and West'.[24] This idea was born out of the tension between increasing apprehension about Soviet ambitions in Europe, and the strengthening of the economic and military ties between Britain and America through the Marshall Plan and NATO. However, with the Czechoslovakian Crisis of 1948, the Berlin Blockade in 1949 and the Korean War in 1950 this prospect disappeared. Soviet cultural directives, as manifested in the Composers' Controversy of 1948, were seen in direct opposition to Western ideas of the artist as the embodiment of freedom. In 1953 the AIA was divided between those who feared Soviet ambition, and those who remained committed Socialists: this division marked the end of the AIA.

While the impact of German-speaking exiled artists is most evident in the abstract art and Social Realism movements, other refugee artists had a more individual influence which cannot be underestimated, such as Hans Feibusch's unique contribution to mural painting in Britain, which we have already examined. Others had an important influence on photography, such as László Moholy-Nagy, and on press photography, such as Karl Hutton, Tim Gidal and Felix Man.

What cannot be denied is that it was a period of intense artistic activity in Britain, stimulated to an inestimable extent by émigré artists.

1. Hans Feibusch in an interview with the author, 21 March 1995

2. Ibid

3. See D. Grimm et al, 'The Works of Art in *Entartete Kunst*, Munich 1937. Artist's Biographies', in Stephanie Barron (ed.), *'Degenerate Art': The Fate of the Avant-Garde in Nazi Germany*, Los Angeles, County Museum of Art exh.cat., 1991, p.232

4. M.-A. von Lüttichau, 'Entartete Kunst, Munich 1937: A Reconstruction', in Stephanie Barron (ed.), op.cit.

5. Hans Feibusch, 'Mein Leben', in *Hans Feibusch: Ein Frankfurter Maler*, Frankfurt, Historisches Museum exh.cat., 1986, p.16

6. P. Thoene, *Modern German Art*, Harmondsworth, 1938; C. Frowein, *Bildende Künstler im Exil in Großbritannien 1933-45*, Frankfurt, 1993, p.22

7. H. Read, *Contemporary British Art*, Harmondsworth, 1964, p.20

8. *Kunst im Exil in Großbritannien 1933-45*, Berlin, 1986, p.125

9. Unfortunately, this mural was destroyed when the chapel was demolished

10. M. Day, *Modern Art in English Churches*, London and Oxford, 1984, p.24

11. For example, Martin Bloch exhibited in 1939, and Fred Feigl in 1945

12. Hans Feibusch, *Mural Painting*, London, 1946, p.2

13. Ibid p.22

14. Ibid p.65

15. H. Read (ed.), *Unit One*, London, 1934, p.11

16. Amongst the other contributions to *Circle* by German-speaking émigrés were: 'Art Education and State' by Walter Gropius; 'Light Painting' by László Moholy-Nagy; and 'The New Typography' by Jan Tschichold. See J. Gage, 'Art and Life', in J. Lewison (ed.), *Circle: Constructive Art in Britain 1934-1940*, Kettle's Yard Gallery, Cambridge, 1982, pp.43-6

17. N. Gabo, 'The Constructive Idea in Art', in J. L. Martin, B. Nicholson and N. Gabo (eds), *Circle*, London, 1937, p.6ff

18. H. Moore, 'Stringed Figures 1937-39', in P. James (ed.), *Henry Moore on Sculpture*, London, 1966, p.209

19. Peter Lanyon quoted in A. Lanyon (ed.), *Peter Lanyon 1918-1964*, Newlyn, 1990, p.28

20. See D. Brown, 'Refugee Artists in Britain', *Art and Artists*, April 1984, p.10. There are some exceptions, for instance the Expressionist works of Josef Hermann, Martin Bloch and Jankel Adler, which had an impact on individual British artists such as Robert Colquhoun and Robert MacBryde.

21. R. Mortimer, 'German Artists', *New Statesman and Nation*, July 1938, p.112

22. L. Morris and R. Radford, *The Story of the Artists' International Association*, Oxford, 1983, p.2

23. As Note 1

24. L. Morris and R. Radford, op.cit., p.1

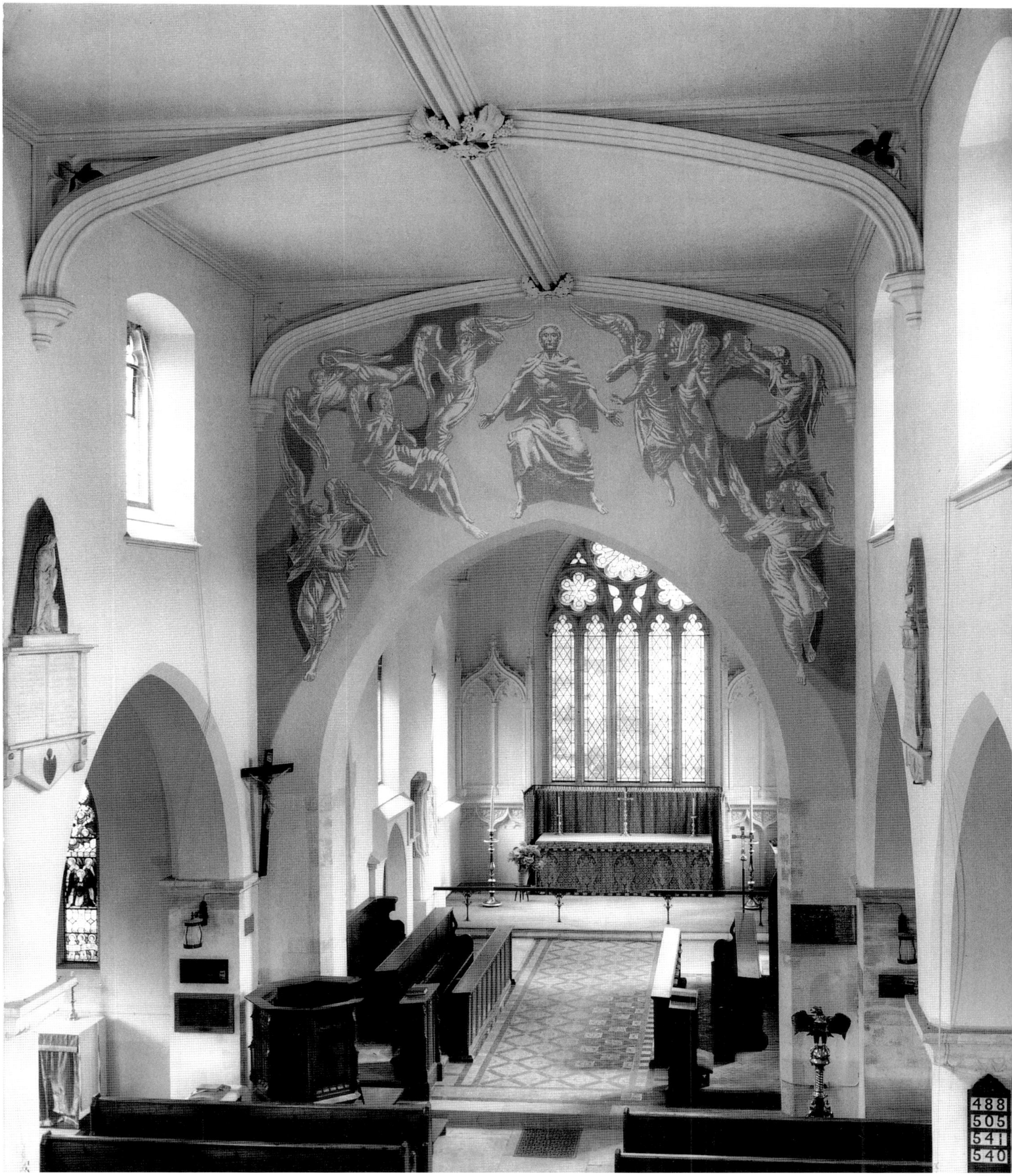

Christ in Majesty 1954
Saint Mary's, Goring-by-Sea, Sussex
M14; Cat.35

The Murals
David Coke

I should like to shake up both architects and painters to overcome the anaemia and whimsicality that have become a characteristic of mural painting, or, at any rate, to keep them in their place in ladies' drawing-rooms and nurseries; but to let churches be decorated by such men as Georges Rouault or Graham Sutherland, in whom there is fire.

Hans Feibusch, *Mural Painting*, 1946, p.29

There is another danger against which I would like to warn Church authorities, architects, painters and sculptors: that of talking baby language. To see the way some of our best church and cathedral builders decorate their work with nursery emblems, golden stars, chubby Christmas angels, lilies, lambs and shepherds, insipid sculpture and paintings of a silly, false naivety, one wonders in what world they live. The men who came home from the war, and all the rest of us, have seen too much horror and evil; when we close our eyes terrible sights haunt us; the world is seething with bestiality; and it is all man's doing. Only the most profound, tragic, moving, sublime vision can redeem us. The voice of the Church should be heard loud over the thunderstorm; and the artist should be her mouthpiece, as of old.

Hans Feibusch, *Mural Painting*, 1946, pp.91–2

In the early 1930s, while he was still in Frankfurt, Feibusch and the group of artists with which he was associated, the *Frankfurter Künstlerbund*, were given the task of designing a series of murals around eight subjects. Whilst working on the sketches, Feibusch realised he knew nothing about the techniques and procedures involved, so he set out to learn. After his arrival in England Feibusch painted a number of small murals for private houses, encouraged by such architects as Sir Charles Reilly, E. Maxwell Fry and Frankland Dark.

His first church commission, *Footwashing* (1938), for the new Methodist Chapel in Colliers Wood High Street, London, for a fee of £50, came to the notice of Dr George Bell, Bishop of Chichester, and led to several major commissions for Dr Bell's diocese. Around twelve of Feibusch's mural projects came through the architect Thomas F. Ford FRIBA, who specialised in the restoration of bombed churches after the war. Ford disliked and distrusted foreigners, particularly Jews, so he was 'difficult' with Feibusch for some time before he had a sudden change of heart and came to like both the artist and his work.

The artist was assisted in his work for many years by Phyllis Bray (1911–91), an artist in her own right and, according to Feibusch, 'never afraid of climbing high and often precarious scaffoldings to work on church walls, ceilings and cupolas'.[1]

From Feibusch's own writings, in particular the trail-blazing book *Mural Painting* of 1946, it can be seen that he was very well aware of the historical tradition within which he was working, as well as of recent developments in the work of his European and British contemporaries. He was not content, however, with the *status quo*, always pleading the case for a direct and true collaboration between architects and painters in the commissioning of murals, and always searching for new means of expressing his subjects.

1. Hans Feibusch in *Hans Feibusch: An Eightieth Birthday Exhibition*, Greater London Council exh.cat., 1978

Hans Feibusch: Mural Painter
Eric Newton

This article was originally published in *Studio*, March 1949.

In one sense I find myself at a disadvantage writing in Venice about a mural painter who has worked mainly in England. For sixteenth-century Venice is not likely to be surpassed in the confidence and magnificence of her mural painting, least of all by twentieth-century England. On the other hand there is something to be said for considering Hans Feibusch's recent mural work with the memory of Veronese's *Apotheosis of Venice* fresh in one's memory. There are not many serious artists today who are anxious to work on a large scale, and the greatest compliment one can pay them is to judge them by the highest standards. Naturally, judged by those standards, they are at once seen as relatively minor figures, but the proof of their seriousness is that they would rather seem so than be acclaimed one-eyed kings in the country of the blind.

But there is another and more valid reason for thinking of Hans Feibusch in the same terms as the giants of the Italian High Renaissance. He is, at least, playing their game. He shares – and this could not be said of any other painter alive in England today – their strength and their weakness. And in so far as his achievement is more modest than theirs, his failures are less lamentable and his mannerisms less irritating. The only other artist in this country who is at his best on a heroic scale is Stanley Spencer, who certainly owes nothing to the sixteenth century – that age of graciousness and grand generalisations. He derives from the more vivid, more closely observant, harsher, quainter spirit of the early fifteenth century.

I stress this difference merely in order to assist myself in defining Hans Feibusch's achievement. He has recently completed what is in some ways his most ambitious, though not his most interesting, mural painting – the twenty-seven-foot-long panel that almost fills the space over the high platform at one end of the big concert room in the civic buildings at Dudley. It is a complex, closely-knit design, full of over-life-sized figures. In spite of its complexity, and in spite of a considerable amount of movement – even violent movement – it is neither crowded nor restless. Moreover, Hans Feibusch has properly understood the mural painter's too-often repeated maxim that a wall decoration must not make a hole in the wall. Timid decorators, pedantically regarding that maxim as an inviolable recipe, have stultified themselves by producing flat areas of self-conscious pattern which offer little but a mild stimulus to the eye and none at all to the mind.

The best wall decorators have rarely refused to make full use of a sense of space. Even the gold backgrounds of the Sienese primitives contain a suggestion of infinite depth. Mantegna's carefully designed perspectives

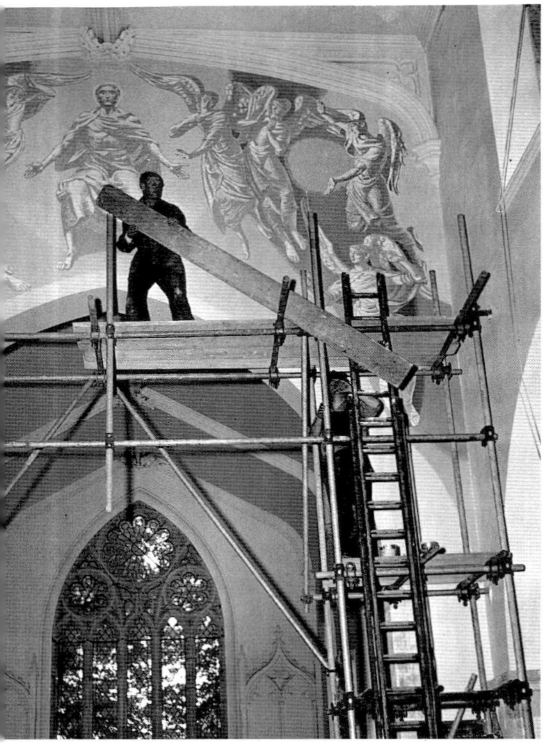

Feibusch at work on *Christ in Majesty* at Saint Mary's, Goring-by-Sea, Sussex, 1954 M14; Cat.35

lead both the mind and the eye on a journey, yet they never defeat the eye's confident sense of an interior enclosed by smooth, solid walls. Feibusch's party of huntsmen at Dudley (the scene depicted is an incident in which the Earl of Dudley's hunting party is interrupted by the King's men) are free to move in any direction they please, towards or away from the spectator as well as *across* the wall space. Yet the whole panel forms a single unit of design. What makes it a satisfying work of art integrated with the wall itself, rather than an enormous portable easel picture which could conceivably be equally at home in another room or another setting, is partly this careful relating of every part to the whole, especially in his colour scheme which provides a continuous texture, and partly his equally careful relation of the whole to its surroundings.

This is perhaps the ultimate test of the good mural painter, that what he does is conceived as *part* of an interior and not as an *addition* to it, so that, once done, the room is inconceivable without it. In two respects Feibusch is a master of this system of visualising his own work as part of a larger whole. He has an unerring sense of scale and a complete understanding of the function of colour. By scale I do not mean merely the actual size of figures and other elements in the design in relation to their architectural setting, but also the treatment of every detail – the weight of each fold of drapery, each clump of foliage, the kind of pattern they make. It is the same problem that a typographer has to solve when, in designing a title page, he selects the size of his letters and the spaces between them and relates them to the page they are to fill, neither dwarfing the page with an excess of weight nor producing an effect of triviality with an insufficiency of it. As for colour, Hans Feibusch has his own very personal method of selecting a strong chord of related colours and balancing them so skilfully that his strict economy of colour is hardly noticed.

These, however, are technical questions. Every artist has to take them into account, in the hope that the spectator will not even notice that he has done so, and that the critic will not dwell on them at the expense of more important considerations. I have only mentioned them in order to stress Feibusch's extraordinary technical competence.

But technical competence, rare though it is, does not always accompany the deeper qualities that one looks for in good painting, though those qualities can never find full expression without it. All art is ultimately illustration, by which I mean that it must have a subject and that the artist must have a very definite attitude to his subject – a 'message', if that is not too pompous a word. And the subject – the narrative element – must always be subordinated to the message. For example, when Feibusch undertook the big processional design in the crypt of St Elisabeth's Church in Eastbourne, he was, naturally, under an obligation to tell the chosen story – the story of Bunyan's *Pilgrim's Progress* – with the utmost clarity and vividness, establishing each stage in the journey of Christian and his wife Christiana so that there could be no doubt about the *kind* of journey, the significance of each adventure and of the final consummation, the arrival, at the east end of the crypt. But that was not enough. There

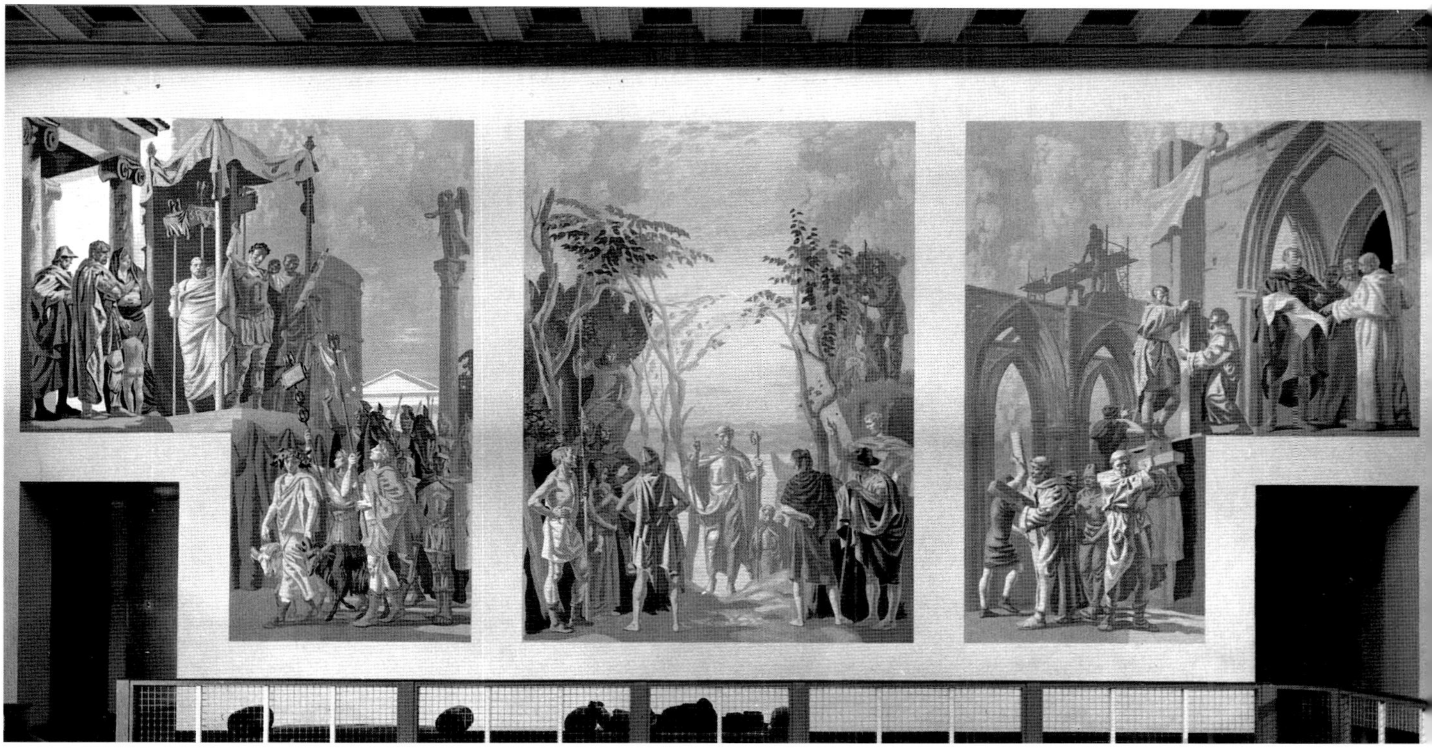

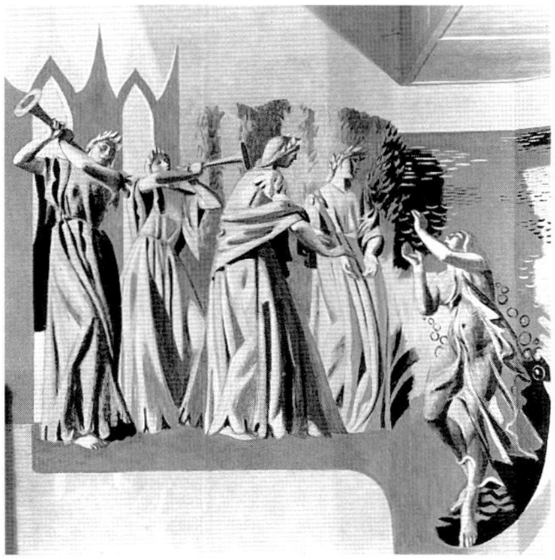

TOP
The History of Newport, one wall of cycle 1961-4. The Civic Centre, Newport, Gwent M35

ABOVE
Pilgrim's Progress (detail) 1944
Saint Elisabeth's, Eastbourne, Sussex
M4; Cats 26, 27, 28

could be a thousand different yet equally clear versions of the story, none of which departed from Bunyan's narrative. One can imagine Van Eyck, Paolo Uccello and Tintoretto each producing an equally valid version: three different attitudes of mind, three different 'messages' brought to bear on the same story. And I have already hinted that Feibusch's attitude is far nearer to that of Tintoretto than to that of the two earlier painters. Therein lies his strength and his weakness as an illustrator. All the grace, the nobility, the visible thrust and counter-thrust of human limbs in movement are there. There is an unfailing suavity of gesture in all he does. Yet he produces it at the expense of other qualities which Van Eyck or Ghirlandaio would certainly have given us. His figures are apt to strike noble attitudes at all costs. Apollo embraces his Daphne a little too elegantly for an ardent lover: Daphne swings her head and extends her arms with such rhythmic harmony that we almost cease to believe in her as a runaway girl. Feibusch shares with the High Renaissance a preoccupation with pure rhythm. He is, above all, a Classic painter, and because of that, the odd, the unexpected is as much beyond his range as the gracious and the heroic is beyond Stanley Spencer's.

I am not blaming him: I am defining him. No painter can have it both ways. The Classic and the Romantic are divided from each other not by deliberate choice but by temperament. But there is enough harshness in the art of today. I like to think that the semi-baroque rhythms of Feibusch may be precursors of a gentler though not a less virile phase in modern painting.

I use the word 'gentler' rather than 'sweeter' advisedly, for Hans

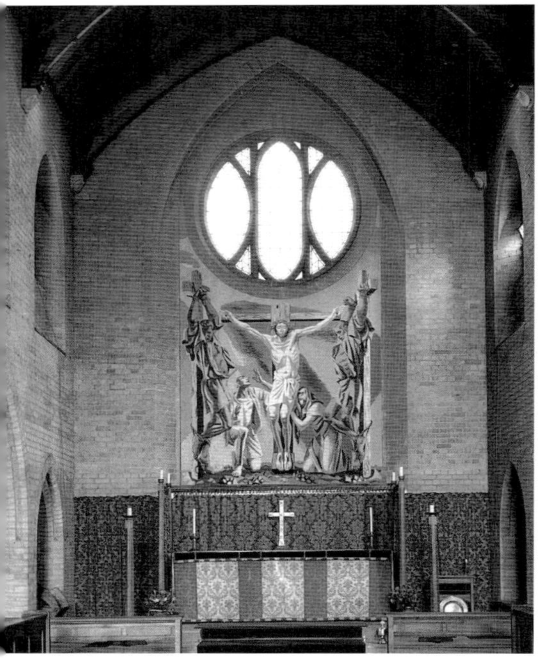

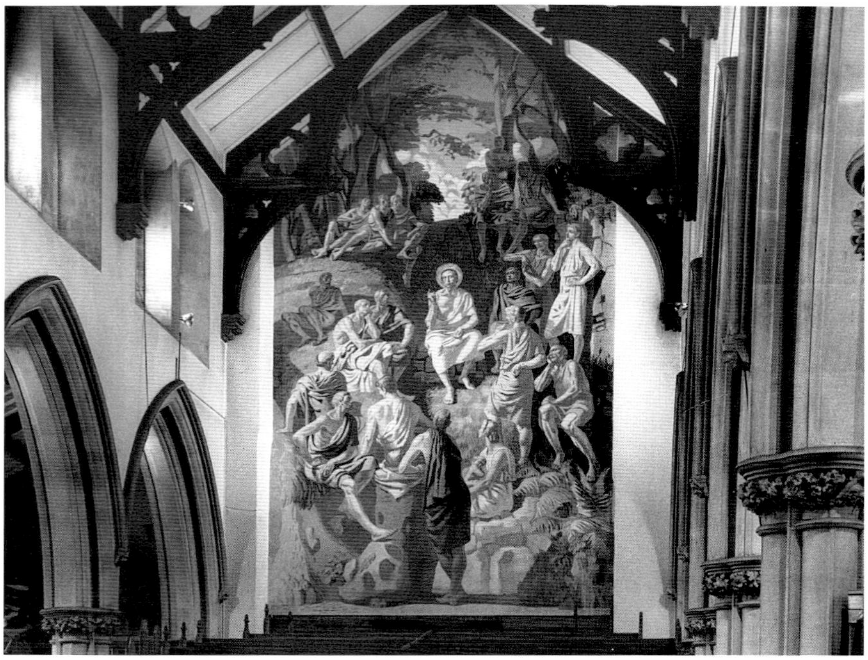

ABOVE
Crucifixion 1948–9
Saint Martin's, Dagenham, Essex
M6

RIGHT
Sermon on the Mount 1956
Saint John the Evangelist, Preston, Lancashire
M18

Feibusch's method of design is too intellectual ever to become sentimental or sweet. Behind it there is a fine discipline in which shape for its own sake is wedded to his own particular brand of humanism. Look, for example, at the basic patches of dark and light in the fresco of two figures half reclining, half floating.[1] They are simple, almost to the point of harshness, and a skilful counterchange of pure draughtsmanship – pale lines on the dark areas, dark lines on the pale – weaves them together and achieves a very subtle balance. The two raised arms, at either end of the panel, frame it vertically, the two extended legs provide horizontals at top and bottom. Or note how, in the single seated figure, four tones, no more, have been used to build up its solid mass.[2] This is the kind of virtuosity that might degenerate into first-class commercial art. Feibusch could easily have been a magnificent poster artist. Luckily he has a heart as well as a head. Apollo and Daphne, Christian and Apollyon are more to him than mere raw material for a decorative scheme.

Possibly that is why he is best when he is most serious, and best, also, when he is most nostalgically excited by the past, especially the pagan past. Even Bunyan's Christian is a Christian of the Mediterranean basin. I doubt whether the prisoner in Bedford gaol had anything like these eloquent rhythmic gestures in mind when he wrote *Pilgrim's Progress*. But then the authors of the Gospels certainly visualised nothing resembling the pictures in the School of San Rocco. Hans Feibusch has plenty of good precedents for accepting the letter of his theme and twisting its spirit to suit his own temperament. What is so heartening is that he twists it in the grand manner, and that therefore he, almost alone among contemporary painters, can be relied on to give seemliness and meaning to the large wall spaces which public buildings, in this age of big-scale planning, are bound to produce.

1. *Lovers*, mural at 2 Strathearn Place, London W2

2. *Apollo*, mural at Sun House, Frognal Way, London NW3

Hans Feibusch and George Bell

Bishop Peter Walker

Bishop Peter Walker was formerly Bishop of Ely (1977–89), and has been a friend of Hans Feibusch for thirty years.

Two small photographs set side by side in a colour album of Hans Feibusch's work, put together to mark his ninetieth birthday: one, a flower still-life, the other, a human study – both invested with a poignancy all their own.

A potted geranium standing beside a vase of peonies and Easter lilies, a soft light suffusing the whole, itself touched with the glow of blue it picks up from the cloth on which, accompanied by a large conch shell competing for attention, the more fragile flowers stand. It is as though a morning's brightness has been caught forever.

Next to it, a head and shoulder portrait of a Pierrot, his whitened face in profile, pensive above his motley as he looks out through the window. What does he see in the world outside?

Underneath, brief details: that the pictures were acquired by the Städel Museum in Frankfurt, Hans Feibusch's native city, one in 1925 and the other in 1927. Six years later they would be gone from public view, their painter proscribed and fled to England.

In time came the artist's consolation, when Hans Feibusch came into the world of Chichester's great Bishop, George Bell – Bell sought him out when a photograph of a Feibusch mural caught his eye in an exhibition at the Tate.[1]

Always modest about his work, Feibusch will not claim for his painting more than a certain competence gained from a very thorough training, and will then perhaps admit to a personal authority in the theory and technique, and indeed the history, of mural painting. But there is more to him than that, and the Bell-Feibusch connection has deeper resonances than merely the timely sympathetic support, offered by a senior Christian churchman, to one artist among many with his life to build again in troubled times. And this deeper question is a live enquiry, for Bishop Bell himself has only just begun to come into his own and be seen as the statesman-bishop and prophetic Christian leader that he was.

What is clear is the instant rapport between these two men. One can reflect on the pleasure Archbishop Runcie's award of the Lambeth Doctorate of Letters to Hans Feibusch in 1985 would have given Bell, and what Bell's nomination, just as he was dying, for the highest honour the German Federal Republic could bestow on an Englishman, the Grand Cross of Merit, must have said to Feibusch, himself to become a Commander of that Order some few years later. But to go deeper, what was it in each man that spoke to the other so immediately, and in the sense of John Henry Newman's *cor ad cor loquitur*? Feibusch's face lights up at the very mention of Bell's name, and one can imagine Bell's own smiling

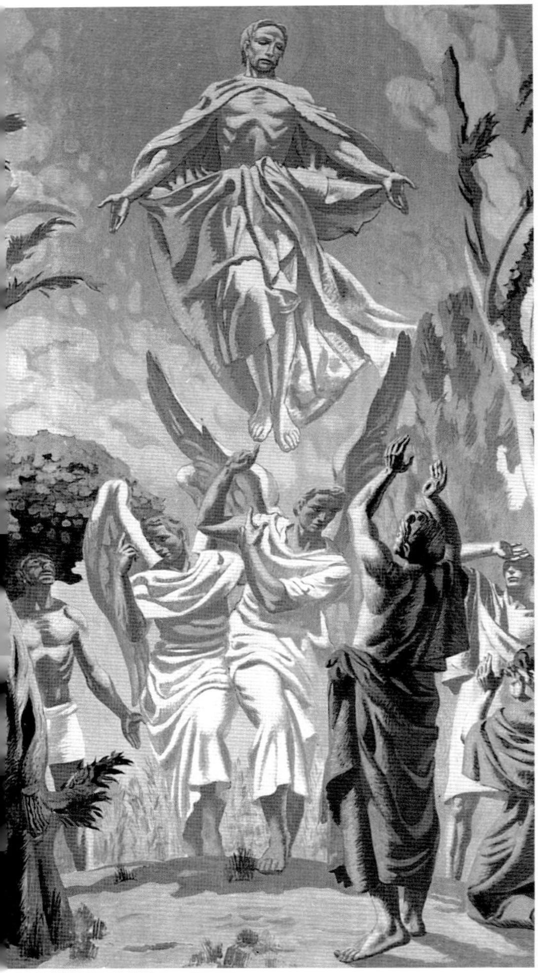

Ascension (detail) 1957
All Saints, Plumstead, London
M21; Cats 39, 40

interest in the present exhibition. What was the root of this deep understanding?

The Presbyterian churchman, Kenneth Slack, summed up in one penetrating phrase the depth of Bell's achievement: 'Bell *saw to the heart* [author's italics] of what was happening in our century' (it was this 'prophetic genius' that had enabled him to see 'to the heart' of events taking place in the Germany of the 1930s under Hitler's Third Reich), 'and he unremittingly called men to a very costly Christian obedience as they faced it.' Which leads me to a Feibusch reminiscence: Hans had come to stay with us in Ely for the first of several visits in my years there as Bishop, and I had taken him out for his first glimpse of the great East Anglian skies. The wide spaces brought back to him the great levels of Eastern Europe where he had seen war service in the Kaiser's army when hardly eighteen, and he then recalled what his Professor of painting had once said of the great painters – not those who painted landscape, but those who depicted their fellow human beings: that Titian painted people as they showed themselves to the world, and Rembrandt, as they might be seen through the loving and the pitying eye of God.

The crucial thing about Hans Feibusch and George Bell together is the catastrophic world they saw facing them, which they were inextricably and crucially men of: they could not, would not, finally look away from the events they beheld as though things were otherwise. Sir William Coldstream's great portrait caught Bell held in this world, his shoulders carrying the weight of his engagement with it, his eyes looking steadily out before him into a middle distance. If Bell was a contemplative, as I think he was, he was so not in the interpretation Eric Kennington's portrait bestows on him, those large eyes looking up into distant heavens, but rather (as is evident in the Coldstream portrait) as one who saw this world with a steady eye, and yet with a compassion – in the Christian perspective of the divine compassion come to earth in Christ – a compassion that can know itself, in human terms, affronted and dismayed and yet made the more resolute by what it sees before it. And Feibusch?

The picture that I recall seeing in Bishop Bell's study in the Palace at Chichester when I saw him for the last time in 1956 was one of Feibusch's powerful lithographs for *The Revelation of Saint John the Divine* (1946), depicting the first angel trumpeter of the Apocalypse launching himself to sound his call: he falls, as it were the first airborne trooper at the moment of free fall, his long trumpet pointed downwards in a powerful diagonal to call down judgement and destruction on the earth. I know no other picture which so dramatically encapsulates the terror of our century. And yet Feibusch has painted on – his great corpus of a lifetime glowing with that vibrancy of colour that has remained distinctly his own. To comprehend this is to find the answer to our original quest for Feibusch's deeper inspiration: that glow is not present in his murals simply to 'brighten up our churches' (although his book on mural painting has words to say on that).

For the articulation of this particular idea I must look to a writer who was herself a woman of this century, Simone Weil. Born, like Hans Feibusch, into a Jewish family of the continent of Europe; born, in fact, only eleven years after him. She died in England in 1943, starving herself in solidarity with the sufferings of her compatriots in Hitler-occupied France. A woman born to know affliction (it is her own particular word for it), feeling herself drawn inescapably to the Christ of the Gospels, but knowing also that she could not in conscience commit herself to the institutional Catholic Church.

A few brief pages of Simone Weil on the *Iliad* of Homer (she was an accomplished classical scholar and teacher) speak immediately to us of our own century for, as she expounds it, the *Iliad* is the great poem of 'Force' (or 'Might'), its subject the suffering of men and women under it. Yet for her the poem is pervaded by one thing that makes it unmatched in Western literature: it is touched throughout by the light (again her own special word) of the poet's tenderness towards the men and women he treats of as so caught in the destructiveness of their world.

I think then of Hans Feibusch's painting *The Footwashing* (1990), whose resonant colour drew admiring attention: here again, as in the flower still-life of 1925, is the Feibusch blue, and glowing against it the brightness of Mary Magdalene's hair. It is the portrayal of a woman's tenderness towards her Lord, caught in the world's relentless cruelty. Or I think of a Feibusch lithograph which I keep in my own room, depicting Adam and Eve expelled from the glow of Eden into the hard blue of the fallen world outside: their look of mutual tenderness as they face it betrays the painter's own sense of human poignancy. Like Bell and his Shakespeare, or Dietrich Bonhoeffer asking from prison for his Greek books, or Simone Weil, Feibusch's inspiration is not an ecclesiastical one in the narrow sense of the word. His graceful bronze *Andromeda* (1986), commissioned for the ship carrying her name, is by one and the same artist who made the *Christus* (1981) which now stands in Ely Cathedral. And he is still painting peonies, and a single sunflower was recently a summer's inspiration.

I look, then, at the glow of Feibusch's *Baptism* (1951) in Chichester Cathedral, proposed to him by Bell, or his mural *Christ in Majesty* (1954) in St Mary's at Goring-by-Sea, whose brilliance was never to be surpassed by him, of the taking of the humanity into God at Christ's Ascension. What do I see if it is not the tenderness felt by an artist for a world of beauty, a world in which human tenderness itself is as fragile as the flowers, but touched, if the Christian message is true, with the glow of God's own love upon it, and God's Yes to it. And that surely was Bell's own inspiration and enduring strength and stay.

1. There are two versions of how George Bell originally met Feibusch. See Jutta Vinzent in this catalogue, p.10.

The Principal Murals of Hans Feibusch

This list of murals collates all information available to date; it may not be comprehensive. If any readers can correct or add to it in substance or detail, please inform Pallant House.

M1 *Footwashing* 1938
Methodist Chapel, Colliers Wood, London SW19
The Chapel has since been demolished and the panel lost.
(For sketches see Cats 23, 24)

M2 *Nativity* 1940–1
Saint Wilfrid's, Elm Grove, Brighton
A triptych commissioned by Bishop Bell in 1939. The church was closed in 1980, but the mural (on three walls of the Lady chapel) still exists. Feibusch painted this mural in gratitude for his shelter in England from the Nazi oppression.
(For sketch see Cat.25)

M3 *Figures from Classical Myths and Legends* early 1940s
Portmeirion Village, Penrhyndeudraeth, Merionethshire
A series of at least four decorative murals painted for the architect Clough Williams-Ellis, of whom Feibusch made a sculpted portrait head in 1977 (Cat.79). There also exists a painting by Feibusch of Clough Williams-Ellis 'apologising' for his architectural sins to Christopher Wren, John Vanbrugh and Nicholas Hawksmoor.
Illus: Hans Feibusch, *Mural Painting*, 1946, pl.XXVI; Christopher Hussey, *Portmeirion still further Explained*, 1946, Figs 30, 59, 61

M4 *Pilgrim's Progress* 1944
Saint Elisabeth's, Victoria Drive, Eastbourne, Sussex
A large mural on three walls of the crypt (14 × 7.9 m). It appears that the commission came through Professor Sir Charles Reilly, who encouraged Feibusch to put himself forward in October 1943. Feibusch was assisted in the work by students of The Eastbourne School of Art. It is now proposed that the Church (designed by P. D. Stonham & Son and A. R. G. Fenning 1931–4) should be demolished: this would certainly mean the destruction of Feibusch's mural.
Illus: *Studio*, June 1948, p.178; *The Artist*, February 1947, pp. 134, 136
Lit: Hans Feibusch, *Mural Painting*, 1946, pp.81–3. Illus: pl.XL
(For sketches see Cats 26, 27, 28)

M5 *Circus Folk* 1948
Temporary murals for the tea pavilion of the *Britain Can Make It* exhibition at the Victoria and Albert Museum.
Illus: *Studio*, March 1949, pp.76–7

M6 *Crucifixion* 1948–9
Saint Martin's, Dagenham, Essex
Dedicated by the Revd C. B. Mortlock on 24 July 1949.
Illus: *Studio*, December 1949, p.192

M7 *A Medieval Hunt* 1948
The Town Hall, Dudley, West Midlands
Lit: *Studio*, March 1949, pp.74–9. Illus: p.74

M8 *The Return of the Prodigal Son* 1950
All Saints, Iden, Sussex
Not strictly a mural, as it is painted in oil on canvas (1.6 × 2 m), but site-specific nevertheless.
Exh: *Sixty Painters for '51*, Arts Council Exhibition. Illus: pl.18 of exh. cat.
(For sketch see Cat.29)

M9 *Baptism of Christ* 1951
The Cathedral of the Holy Trinity, Chichester, Sussex
Commissioned directly by Bishop Bell in 1950 and originally intended to mask a disused doorway, although it was moved to the adjacent west wall in 1977.
Lit: Hans Feibusch, 'Mural Paintings in Churches', in *Studio*, April 1954, p.106 (the illustration shows the mural in its original setting); Mary Hobbs (ed.), *Chichester Cathedral: An Historical Survey*, Chichester, 1994, pp.268–9, pl.XXI
(For sketches see Cats 30, 31, 32, 33)

M10 *Crucifixion* 1951
Festival Church of Saint John, Waterloo Road, London SE1
One of the commissions that came to Feibusch from the architect Thomas F. Ford, who restored and redesigned the church, and planned the mural. The mural is in a niche over the high altar, which is itself decorated by *Virgin and Child with Saints and Angels*, also by Feibusch.
Lit: As M9, p.108. Illus: p.109

M11 *Adoration of the Magi* 1952
Saint John the Baptist, Egham, Surrey
Painted in a specially erected shallow niche over the high altar.
Lit: As M9, p.106. Illus: pp.106, 107

M12 *Christ Appearing to the Disciples* 1952
The Holy Name Chapel, All Hallows, Wellingborough, Northamptonshire
Painted in a niche over the altar.

M13 *Ascension* 1953
Bishop's Palace Chapel, Chichester, Sussex
A direct and private commission from Bishop Bell. Painted on the west wall, which is interrupted by a Victorian organ and a Tudor window.
Lit: As M9, p.107. Illus: p.108

M14 *Christ in Majesty* 1954
Saint Mary's, Goring-by-Sea, Sussex
The west face of the chancel arch.
(For sketch see Cat.35)

M15 *Ascension* 1955
Saint Mary's, Grove Road, Welling, Kent
Above the high altar.
Illus: *Pilgrims' Way*, November 1971: cover picture of the artist at work on the mural.
(For sketch see Cat.36)

M16 *A Flight of Angels* 1955-6
Saint Michael and All Angels, Paulsgrove, Portsmouth
A scalloped oval ceiling decoration with angels and clouds against a blue sky.

M17 *The Temptation of Christ* 1956
Saint Michael and All Angels, Paulsgrove, Portsmouth
Above the altar.

M18 *Sermon on the Mount* 1956
Saint John the Evangelist, Preston, Lancashire
The mural is on the upper part of the west wall; it measures approximately 6 × 4 m. The subject is the Beatitudes (Matthew 5. i-x).

M19 *The Ascension* 1956-7
Church of the Ascension, Preston Road, Harrow, Middlesex
In a tall narrow niche over the high altar.

M20 *Resurrection Triptych* 1957-8
Saint James's, Martin Way, Merton, London SW20
Above the altar.
(For sketch see Cat.37)

M21 *Ascension* 1957
All Saints, Herbert Road, Plumstead, London SE18
Above the altar.
(For sketches see Cats 39, 40)

M22 *Resurrection and Scenes from the Life of Saint Peter Triptych* 1957
Saint Peter's, Pickford Lane, Bexleyheath, Kent
The central Resurrection composition is closely related to that at Saint James's, Merton. Feibusch also decorated the church's shallow cupola.
(For sketch see Cat.38)

M23 *Ascension* 1957
Church of the Ascension, The Avenue, Wembley

M24 *Christ Breaking through the Clouds of Sin* 1957
Saint Barnabas, Rochester Way, Eltham, London SE9
On the apse ceiling.

M25 *Noli Me Tangere* 1957-8
All Hallows, Union Street, Southwark, London SE1
This mural, above the altar, has been walled up 'for protection' so is now inaccessible.
(For sketches see Cats 42, 43)

M26 *Christ in Glory* 1957-8
Saint Sidwell's, Sidwell Street, Exeter, Devon
A large mural on the east wall of the church, in which the artist has portrayed himself and his family in the lower left.
(For sketch see Cat.41)

M27 *Angels and Saints* 1958
Saint Michael and All Angels, Bishop Ken Road, Harrow Weald, Middlesex
East wall, behind the altar.

M28 *The Last Judgement* 1958
Christ Church and Saint Stephen, Candahar Road, Battersea, London SW11
East wall.
Feibusch also painted a second mural for the baptistry in this church, *Angels with Children*.

M29 *Saint Crispin Handing out Shoes* 1959
Saint Crispin's, Southwark Park Road, Bermondsey, London SE16
In a shallow niche above the altar.

M30 *Ascension* 1959
Saint Vedast's, Foster Lane, London EC2
East wall, above the altar.
Feibusch also executed a mural of *A Seated Figure with Angels in a Landscape* for the rectory at Saint Vedast's. This mural was commissioned by Canon C. B. Mortlock, previously Treasurer of Chichester Cathedral.

M31 *Baptism of Christ* 1960
Old Saint George's Baptist Church, Catherine Street, Plymouth, Devon
Over the altar.
(For sketch see Cat.44)

M32 *Crucifixion* 1960
Holy Trinity, Rotherhithe, London SE16

M33 *Crucifixion Triptych* 1962
Saint Ethelburga the Virgin within Bishopsgate, London EC2
Over the altar.
The mural was destroyed along with the church by a terrorist bomb in the summer of 1993.
(For sketch see Cat.45)

M34 *Christ in Glory* 1963
Saint Mark's Chapel, Coventry and Warwickshire Hospital, Coventry, West Midlands
On the east wall.

M35 *The History of Newport* 1961-4
The Civic Centre, Newport, Gwent
A series of twelve large murals (each over 6 metres high) around the Central Hall of The Civic Centre, commissioned by The Newport Borough Council in 1960, with the help of a grant from The Edwin Austin Abbey Memorial Trust Fund for mural painting in Great Britain. The artist, sixty-three at the time, was assisted in this scheme by Phyllis Bray, who painted the landscape settings.

M36 *The Trinity in Glory* 1965-6
Saint Alban the Martyr, Holborn, London EC1
The mural (8.84 × 15.25 m) covers the east wall of the church, above the altar. The church, designed by Sir Giles Gilbert Scott, was consecrated in 1961. Feibusch, who was assisted in this, his loftiest mural, by Phyllis Bray, had the pigments specially created as oil paints by Winsor and Newton.
Illus: *Church Building*, Whitsun 1985, p.18
(For sketches see Cats 46, 47)
In 1969-70 Feibusch also painted a major series of fourteen *Stations of the Cross* (in oil on canvas) for Saint Albans, which were marouflaged to the north and south walls of the church.
(For sketches see Cats 48, 49, 50)

M37 *Everyman as a Traveller* 1966
The Little Theatre (also known as the Dolman Theatre), Newport, Gwent

M38 *Christ in Glory* 1967
Priory Church of the Holy Trinity, Christchurch, Dorset
Above the reredos in the Great Quire.

M39 *Five Stories from the Old Testament* 1973
Stern Hall, 33 Seymour Place, London W1

Murals for private houses include:

*Diana and Actaeon c.*1934
11 Wellington Square, London SW3
For James Laver (architect Frankland Dark)

Sea Creatures 1938
Petworth Cottage, Bosham, Sussex
(For sketch see Cat.13)

Apparition n.d. (1930s/1940s)
Westminster Court, London NW8
Illus: *Studio*, March 1949, p.79

Apollo, Dionysos and a Leopard and *Helios* n.d. (1930s/1940s)
Sun House, Frognal Way, London NW3
For P. Goodbrook (architect E. Maxwell Fry)
Illus: *Studio*, March 1949, p.78

Apollo and Pan n.d. (1930s/1940s)
Dining Room, Dorchester Hotel, Park Lane, London W1
(architect Frankland Dark)
This mural has now been painted over.

Lovers n.d. (1930s/1940s)
2 Strathearn Place, London W2
Illus: *Studio*, March 1949, p.78

Ancient Fantasies c. 1974
For a house in Bath. A cartoon and some sketches dated 1974 exist at the studio.

Regarding Hans Feibusch

Just because one can draw an apple or paint a landscape, it does not mean one is of the same ilk. Though both Feibusch & I are a deft hand at such disciplines, we are quite different, & this being so, I am able to pretend to be objective & appreciate the art of Hans Feibusch.

Hans Feibush the artist, who has contributed such a body work, so many lovely paintings & some are exhibited in this show, here at Chichester. He is continuing to work with the greatest dedication, though his eyesight is getting poor, he has taken to sculpture as an alternative to painting A good tradition this, Just look at Degas, who when blindness threatened him, he had to abandoned the easel, & modelled with some effect: a group of Ballerinas some art lovers feel that they even excell the quality of his paintings

Facsimile of an appreciation of Hans Feibusch written by fellow artist Hans Tisdall in April 1995

2

Feibusch appears to veer in likewise direction & is modelling some splendid portraits. He also sculpted a lifesize statue of St John the Baptist, outside of St John's Wood Church in London

You may be wondering why I refer to our artist hero Brusky as Feibusch? this is due to the curio that both of us have the same pre nom Hans. This at times leads to a mix up of identity & work & requires some explanations. I, unlike Feibusch, have never made an eclesiastic picture. whilst he never painted a shorescape at Hastings, which was my basic task

A critique of merit artistic & the standing in the charts, would be frivolous & quite inappropriate, for me. Anyhow one Artist musing about another Artist can not be unbiased, however symphatetic. There are lurking sensitive toes, which one is bound to tread upon, & other aesthetic piccadillos which are insurmontable. Sensitive, ever so sensitive...

3 Undoubtedly, one would assume that two artists of German origin & both be called Hans - would be as thick as thieves. Not so, our backgrounds are as different as can be: Feibush comes from a medical family & therefore entered the artschool totally unbiased, chaste. Quite besotted with his need to learn all about, not only ART but how to put his real & thrusting talent to work & paint lovely pictures. At the Berlin academy, he came under the influence of Karl Hofer. This was just the right place for him, to awaken his artistic cravings & Karl Hofer the teacher on whose generous table he partook, has left fragments of influence, which are still evident in Feibusches palette of his beautiful paintings & murals.

Coming back to our origins of contrast. Feibusch had to enter the strange life of artists from square one. Look how splendidly he has succeeded, not only with his dedication to all tasks of integration into a: rare tribe, of vermillion Red & Ultramarine blue. His studiowork soon extended to monumental works for churches. To mention only one: the church of St Ethelburgha in the City of London depicts Christ in the center with Angels on either side. This Church was the victim of an IRA Bomb though mainly destroyed, some fragments of the wallpainting are still extant. Generously the artist promised to restore the work if the church is rebuilt. This is only one of the many Feibusch murals executed for Churches, Public Buildings & municipal & heraldic Places.

I recall these instances of activites only to show, how a man, posessed of talent & an urge to paint, can, without artistic background enter so sucsessfully Bohemia & its varyagated foibles. This I admire enormously.

Since my origins are quite different, I must confess that my parents were both artists & I drank the commotion of artists life & racketeering with my mothers milk, Thus a place for me in the artworld was inevitable. I too have been at work for a life time.

Privately Feibush & I are very friendly without beeing in each others pockets. The artist is a dear man, & a great artist

Hans [illegible] ©
14
II
1995

Hans Feibusch: Colourist
David Coke

Feibusch is, first and foremost, a colourist. He is also (as becomes obvious from this exhibition) a fine draughtsman, technically proficient and an acute observer; but in his art it is colour that does the work, that first attracts the eye and then engages our attention.

The immediate translation of form into colour is an aim towards which many artists strive, and one which Feibusch achieves magnificently. The problem faced by many artists is that of finding a two-dimensional equivalent for the three-dimensional forms around us. It is impossible actually to re-create those forms via painting; it is equally impossible to include all the detail, all the shapes, all the colours. Once a painter has accepted this, and has started to develop from that premise, he can begin to create works of art, as opposed to mere representations.

Painters approach the challenge of creation in many ways. Some avoid figurative representation altogether, others adopt line or texture to define form; light and shade, reflection and refraction, the abstraction of, or emphasis on, particular features, characteristics or details are all equally valid.

At an early stage Feibusch chose colour as his vehicle, and he has remained true to that choice throughout his career. Indeed, the artist's most recent works, created in his ninety-seventh year, use some of the most glowing colours to be seen in any British art of this century.

But enormous experience and a very special skill are needed to handle the many colours of Feibusch's coat. After exploring semi-abstraction in the 1930s, examining the stylisation of figures, and adopting a strictly limited palette, the 1940s see Feibusch give way to a very much more liberal use of colour. The discipline of the early years is replaced by the confidence of maturity.

Colour used in this way is not always easy for the observer to comprehend. Feibusch's work cannot be ignored; we have to take notice of it, but that does not mean that we have to feel comfortable with it. Indeed, many people are, at first, upset or offended by his use of colour. Colour, of course, helps to create mood, it arouses or suppresses emotion, and Feibusch's bold use of it contrasts strongly with traditional views of what constitutes 'tasteful' art.

However, once we open up to these extraordinary works, forget our preconceptions and biases, and allow ourselves to react purely emotionally to the works before us, we discover their real warmth, humanity and vitality.

The basic precepts behind the artist's works are very simple. Colour is an equivalent, a metaphor, for form. The composition is constructed from areas of colour. The particular colours chosen for the subject depicted reflect and express the mood of that subject, whether it be biblical, mythological, landscape, still-life or portrait. Colour also helps us to interpret what we are seeing through basic symbolism – cool earth colours contrasting with warm and bright colours to express a division between the earthly and heavenly areas of a mural.

When we come to compare Feibusch's work with that of his contemporaries in this country, we find ourselves in some difficulty. We will look in vain for any direct influence, whether on Feibusch from outside, or from him upon others. His influences lie in his background: through his teachers, particularly Karl Hofer (1878-1955) and André Lhote (1885-1962) and through his love of Italian art, both historical (Masaccio, Piero della Francesca and Benozzo Gozzoli) and contemporary (Carrà, de Chirico, Morandi), he developed a kind of 'archaic realism' which sometimes comes close to the romanticism of the nineteenth-century painters Feuerbach and Von Marées. The canvas of Feibusch is a crowded one, but crowded only with essential elements; there is no room for incidental or irrelevant detail, there are no distractions.

An artistic equal for the work of Hans Feibusch can be found in the creative output of another German Jew exiled in 1933, who also felt strong Italian influences – Kurt Weill. Indeed, the description of Weill's composition in Grove's *Dictionary of Music and Musicians* (1954) could apply equally to Feibusch: '… lyrical episodes, vivacious rhythms striking a balance between light music and jazz, and on simplified harmonies of harsh forcefulness rather than on the pyrotechnics of the Straussian orchestra.'

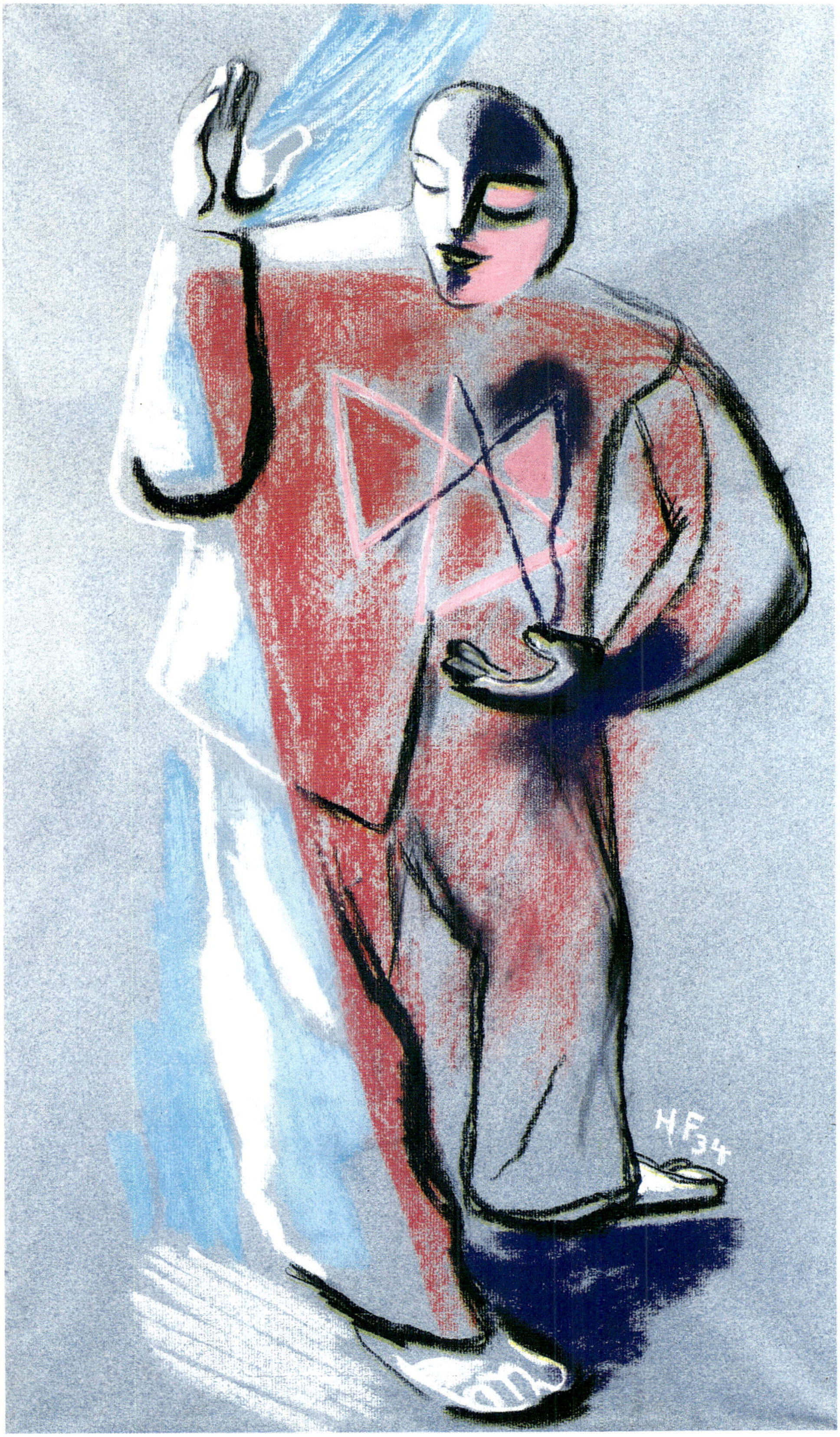

Plate 1
The Magician 1934 (Cat.4)
Chalk and pastel on blue paper
680 × 380 mm

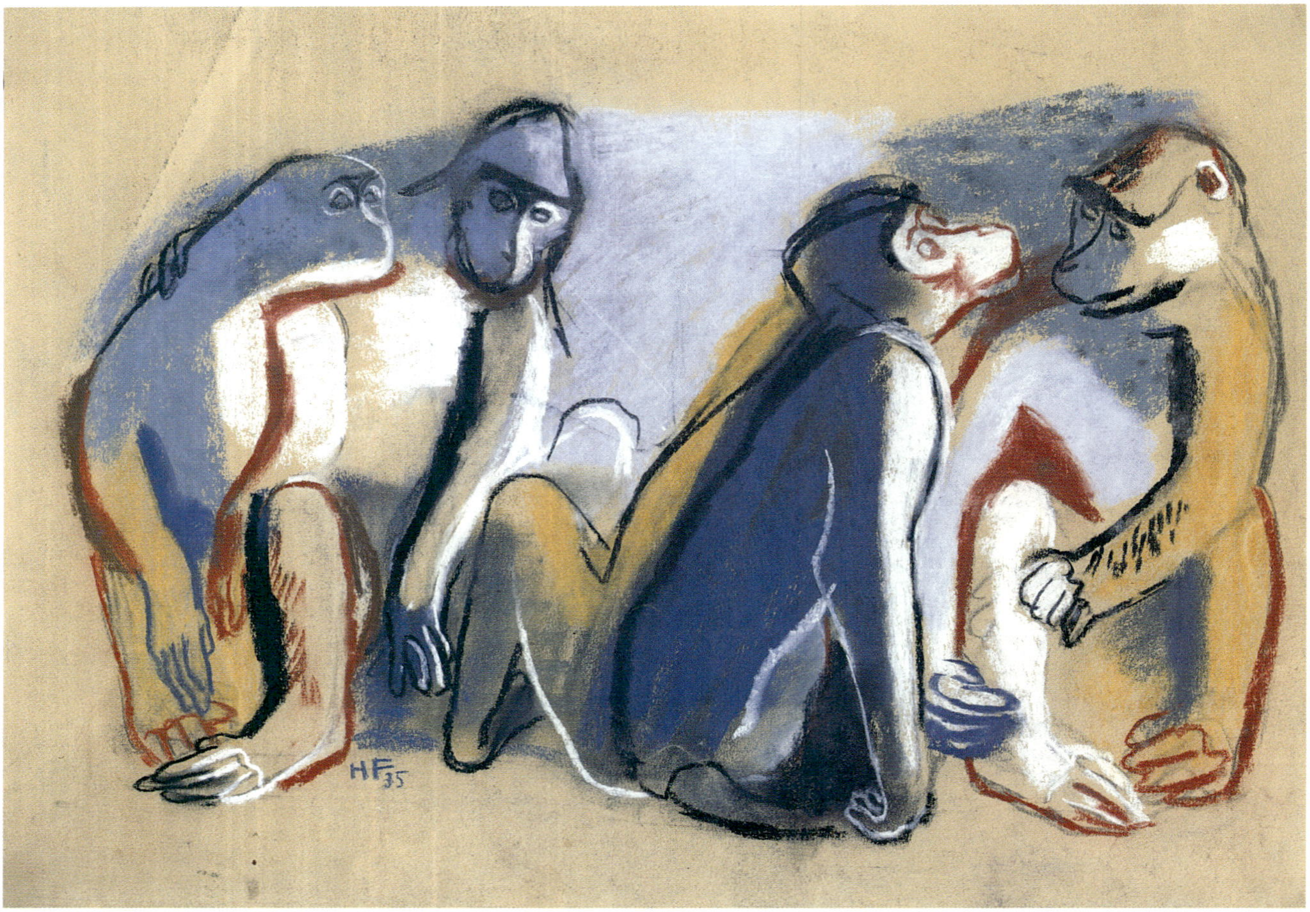

Plate 2
A Group of Apes 1935 (Cat.8)
Chalk and pastel 460 × 630 mm

Plate 3
Latona and the Frogs 1934 (Cat.5)
Chalk and pastel 655 × 495 mm

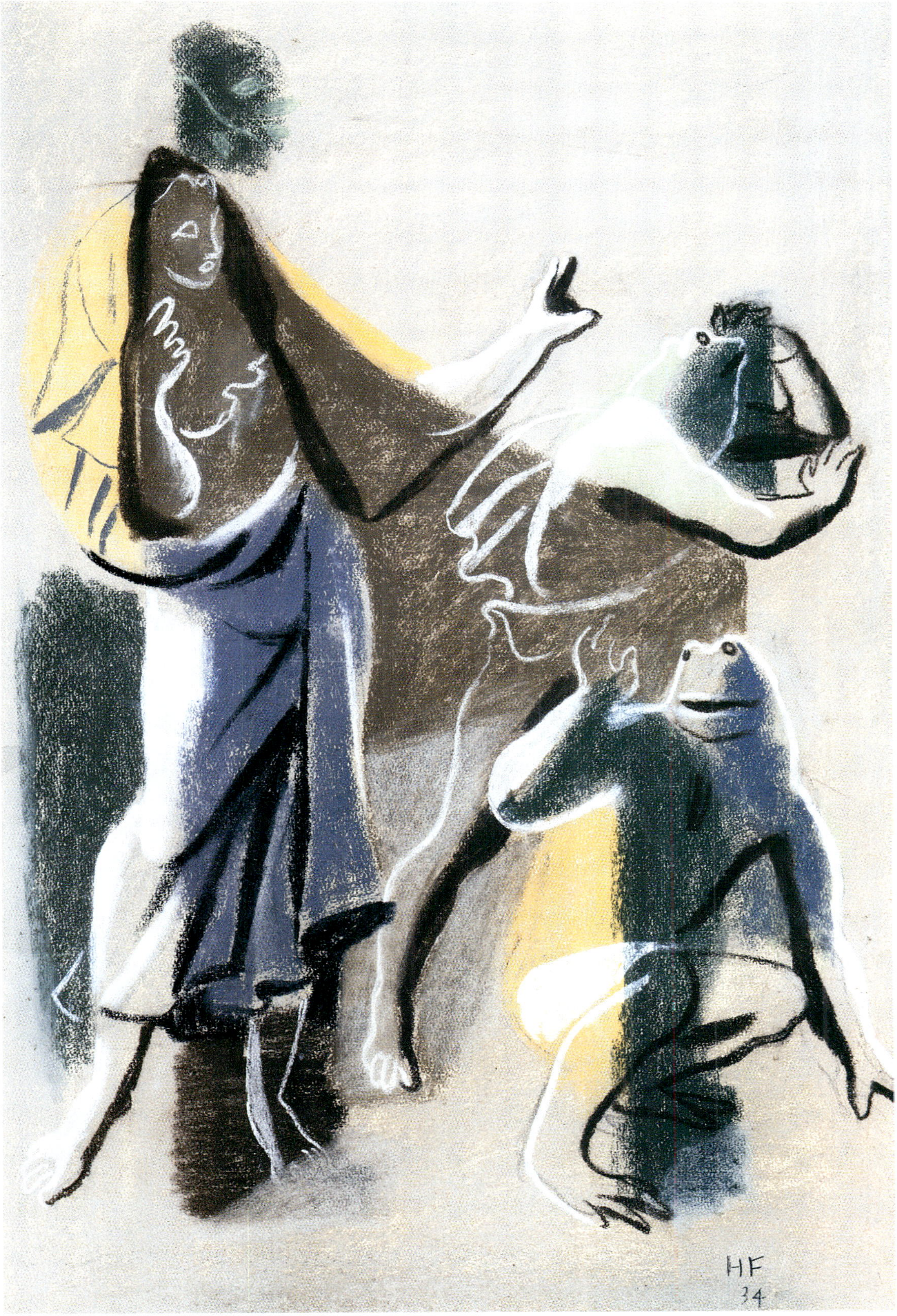

3

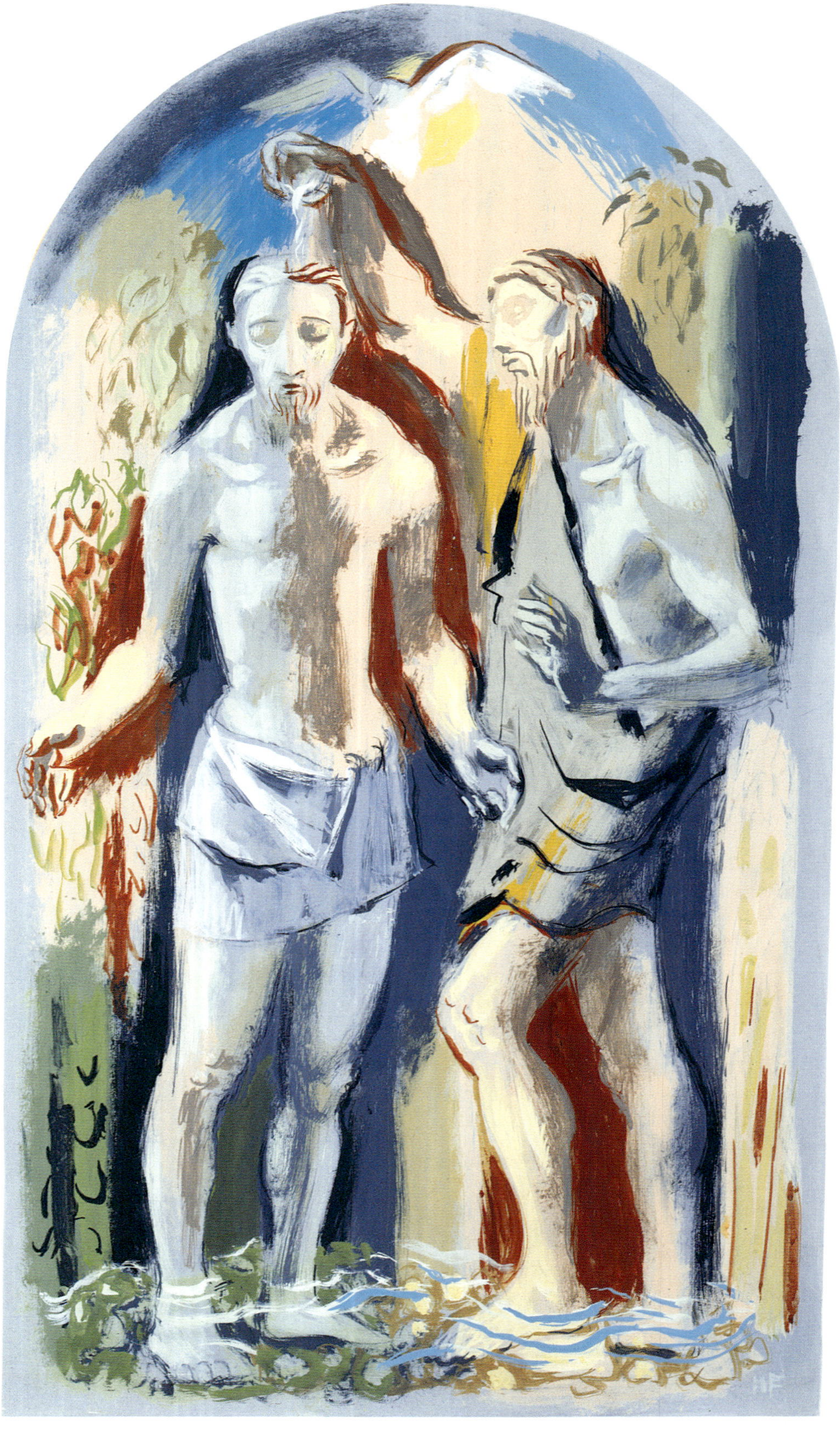

Plate 4
Sketch for *Baptism of Christ*
1950–1
(Cat.33; M9)
Gouache 710 × 410 mm
The mural *Baptism of Christ* is in the Cathedral of the Holy Trinity in Chichester

Plate 5
Sketch for an unidentified mural *Scenes from the Life of Christ* 1952 (Cat.34)
Gouache 454 × 373 mm

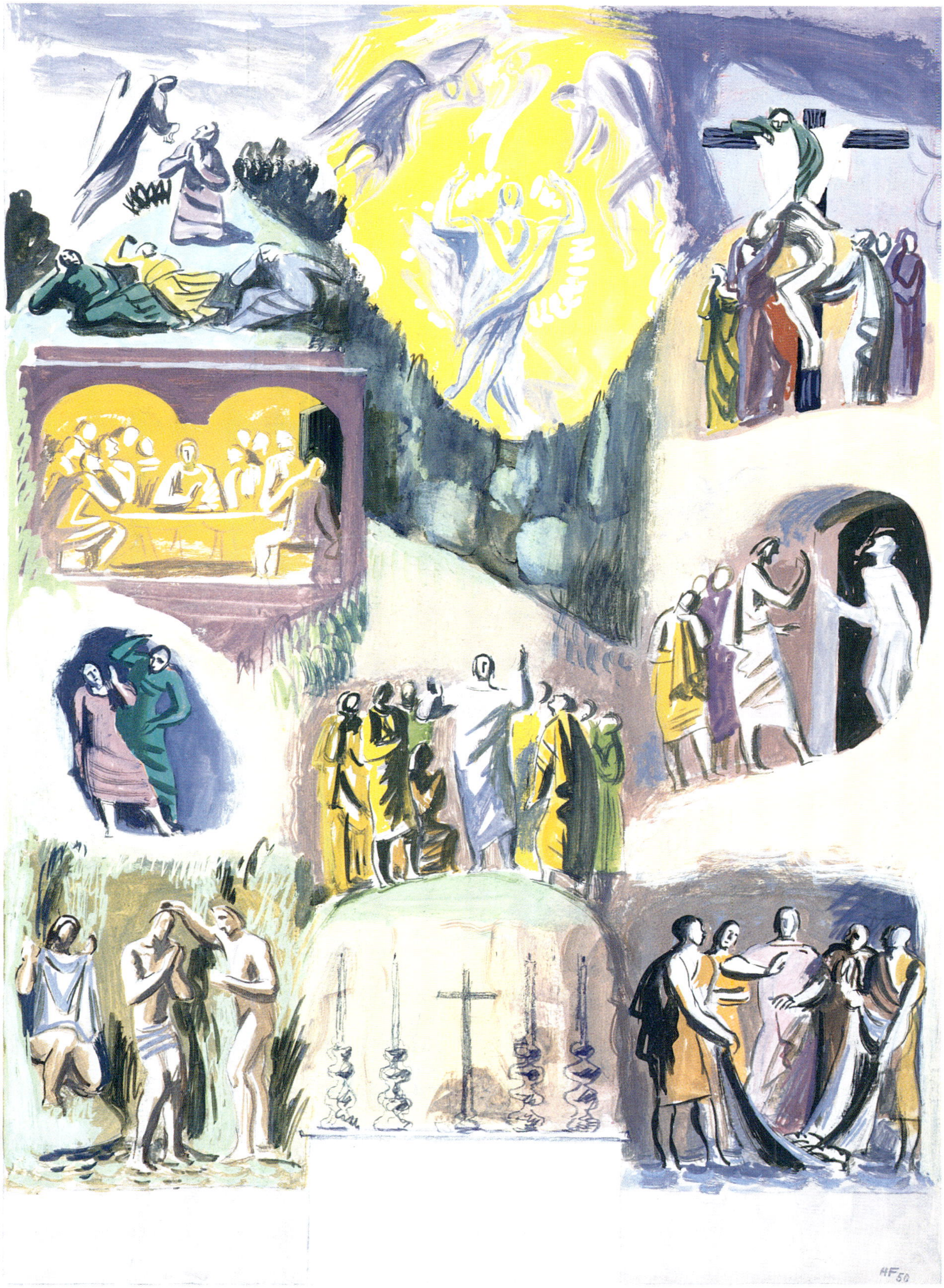

5

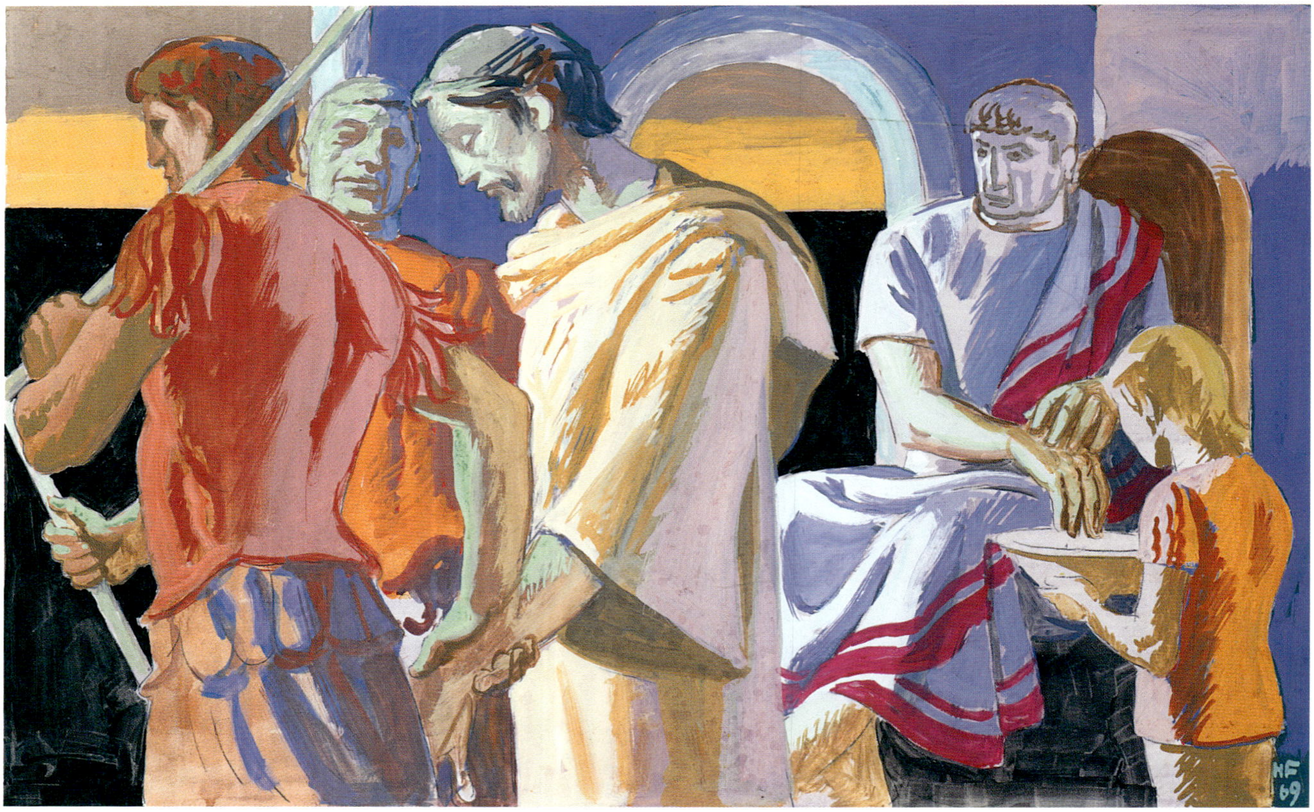

Plate 6
Sketch for *Stations of the Cross I: Christ before Pilate* 1969 (Cat.49; M36)
Gouache 545 × 750 mm
The *Stations of the Cross* are in Saint Alban the Martyr, Holborn, London EC1

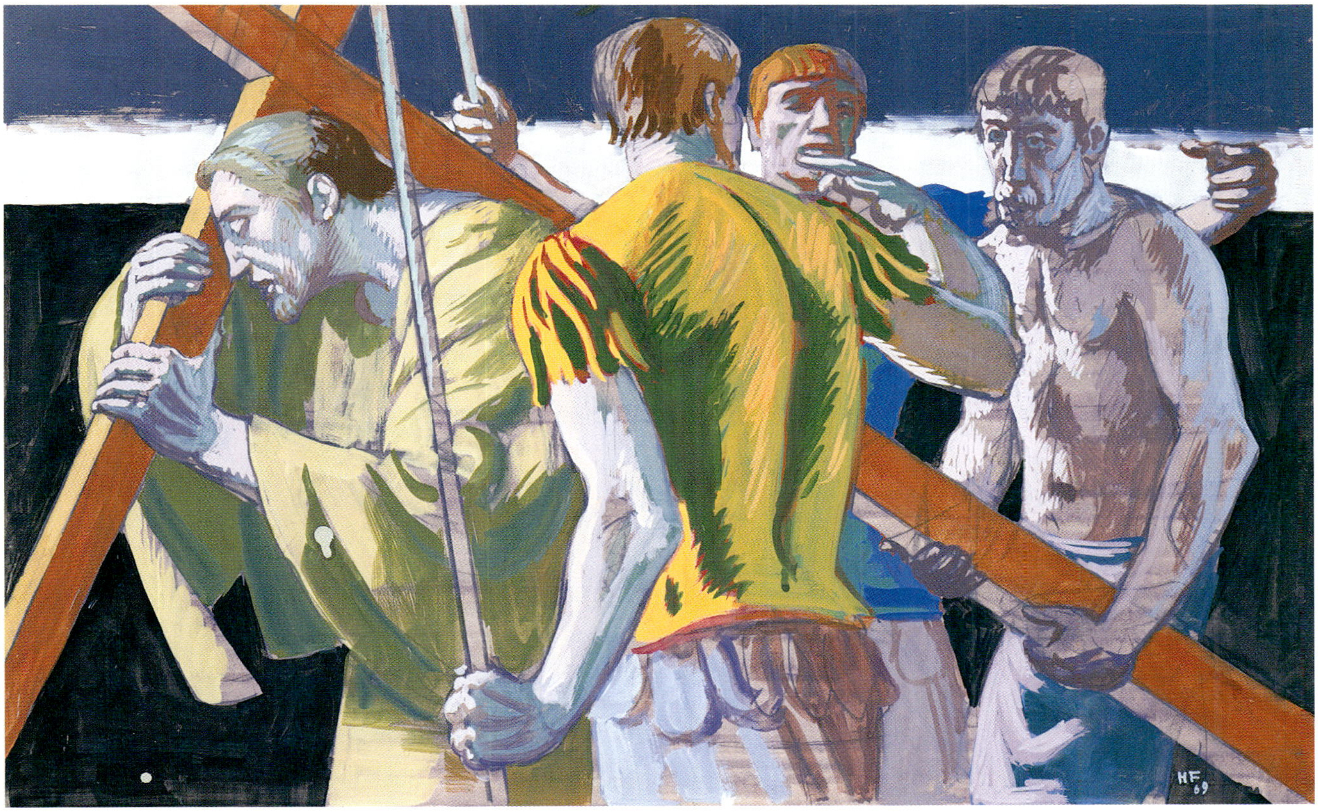

Plate 7
Sketch for *Stations of the Cross V: Christ Carrying the Cross* 1969 (Cat. 50; M36)
Gouache 545 × 750 mm
The *Stations of the Cross* are in Saint Alban the Martyr, Holborn, London EC1

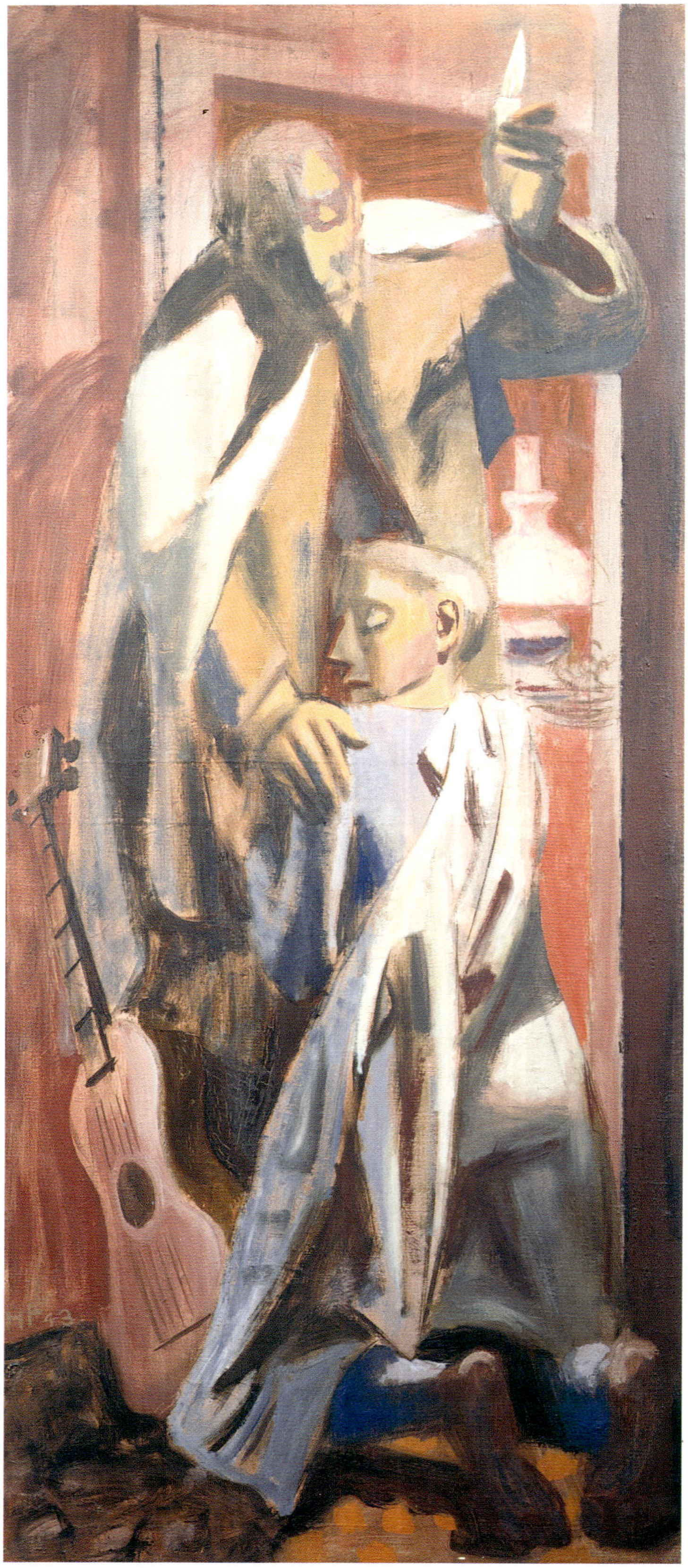

Plate 8
The Prodigal Son 1943 (Cat.54)
Oil on canvas 1525 × 660 mm

Plate 9
Sketch for a mural of *The Ascension* 1992
(Cat.53)
Gouache 680 × 540 mm
Possibly intended for a church in
Tewkesbury, but never executed

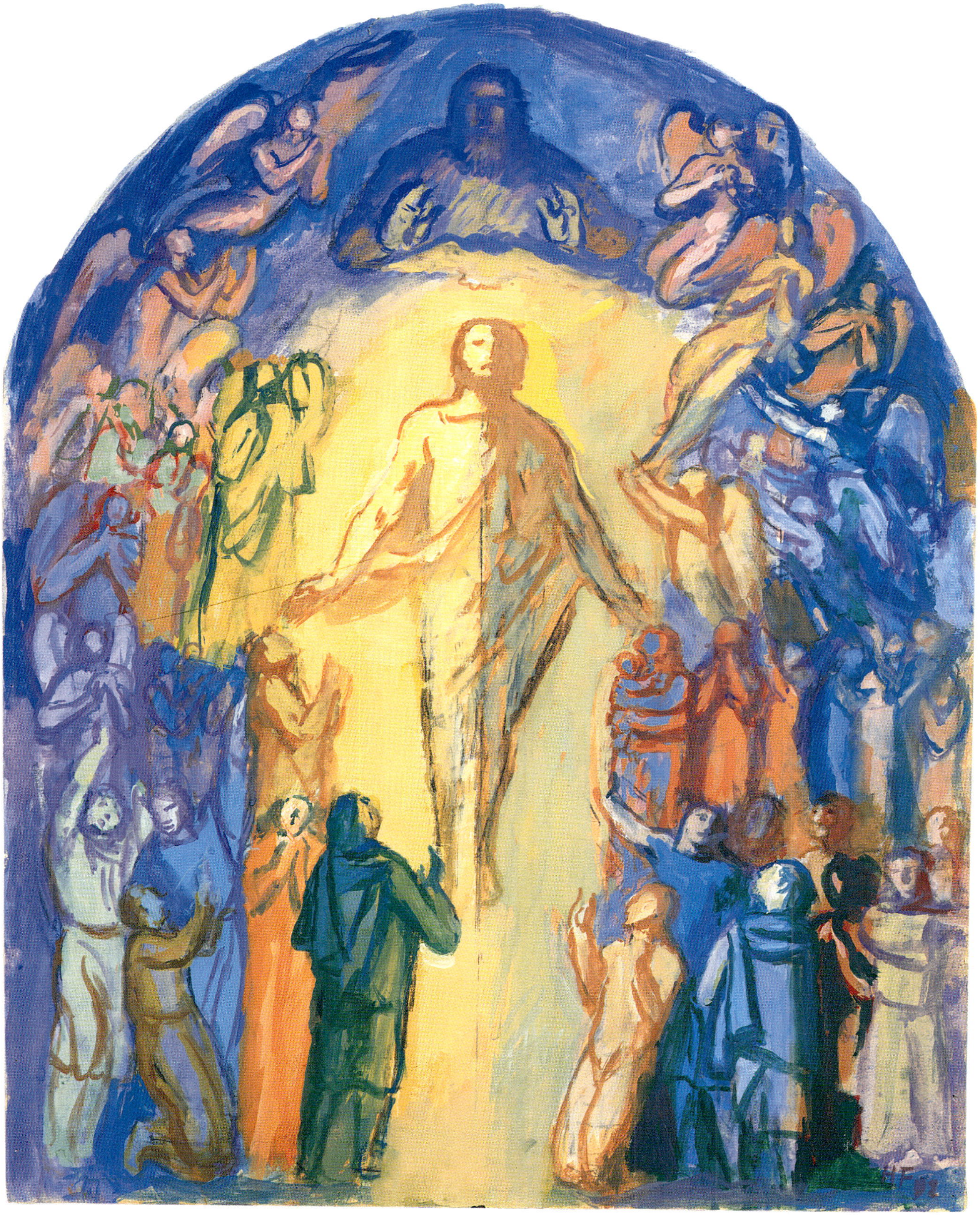

9

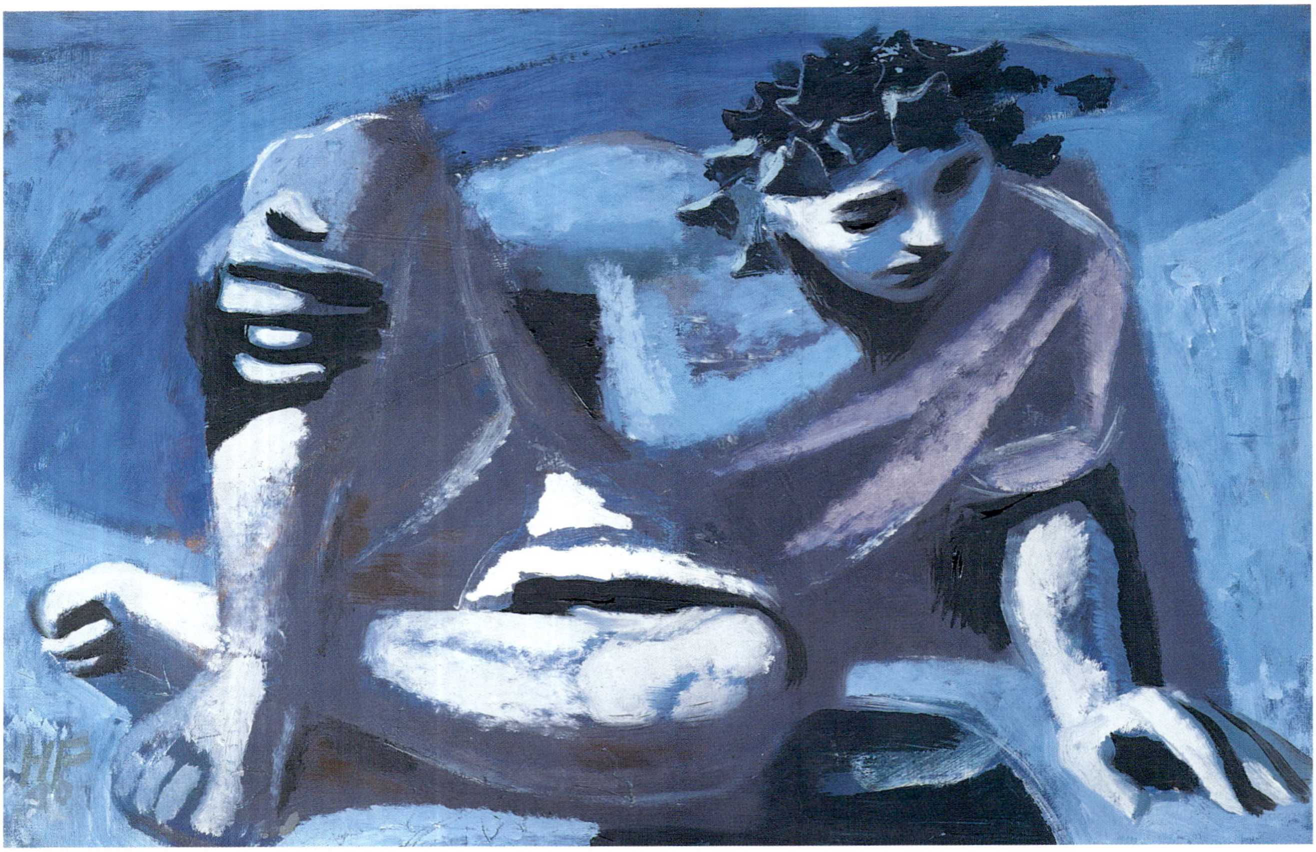

Plate 10
Narcissus 1946 (Cat.55)
Oil on canvas 606 × 915 mm
See also front cover illustration (detail)

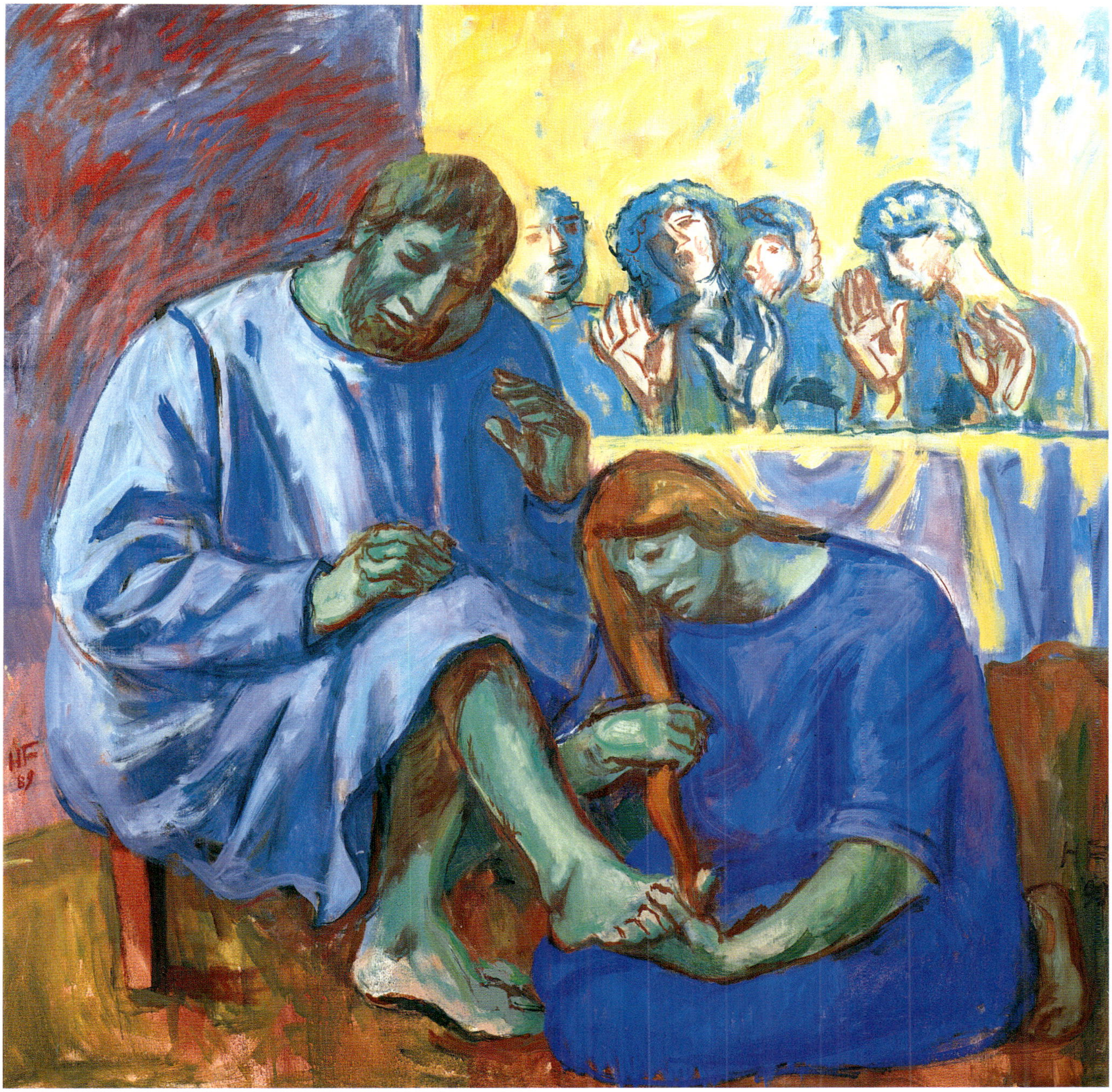

Plate 11
The Footwashing 1990 (Cat.65)
Oil on canvas 1100 × 1100mm

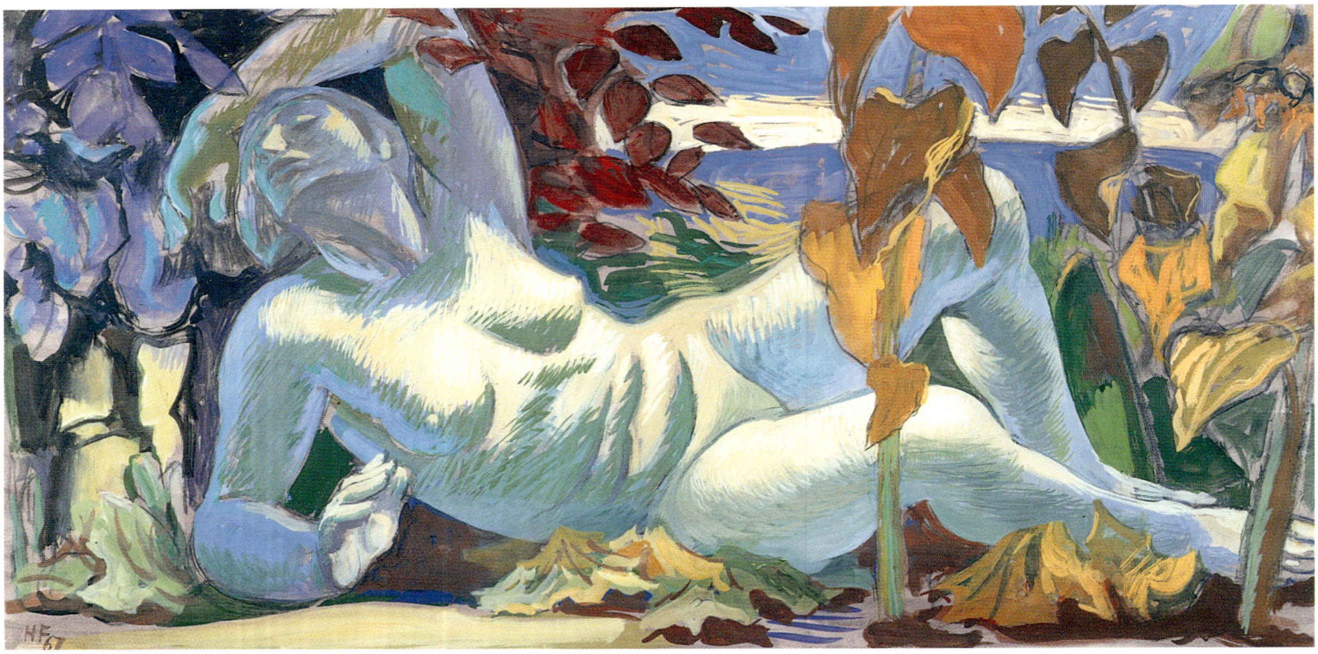

Plate 12
The Four Seasons: Autumn 1967 (Cat.59)
Gouache and watercolour
530 × 1035 mm

Plate 13
The Madonna of the Sunflowers 1984
(Cat.62)
Oil on canvas 1520 × 1065 mm
See also Cat.51 for preparatory sketch

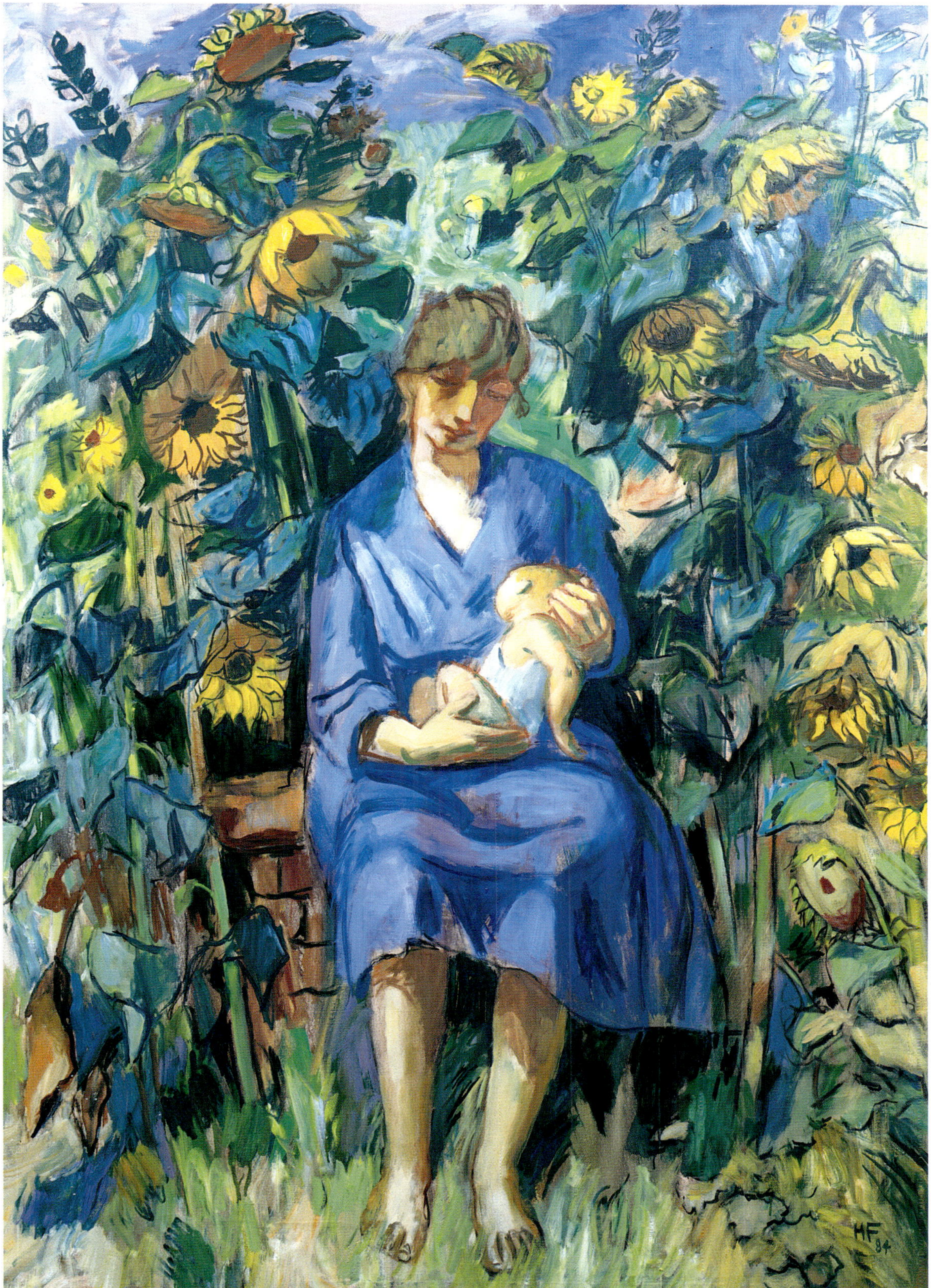

13

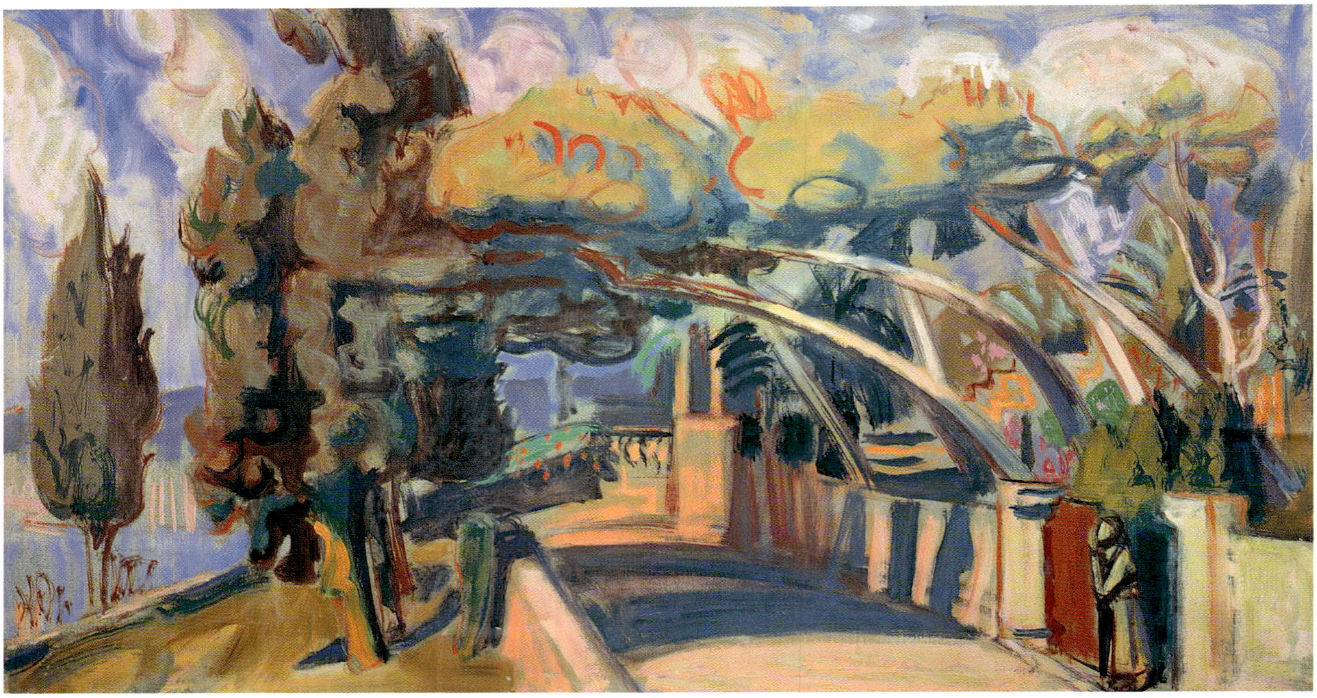

Plate 14
The Bent Trees, Taormina 1952 (Cat.74)
Oil on canvas 505 × 920 mm

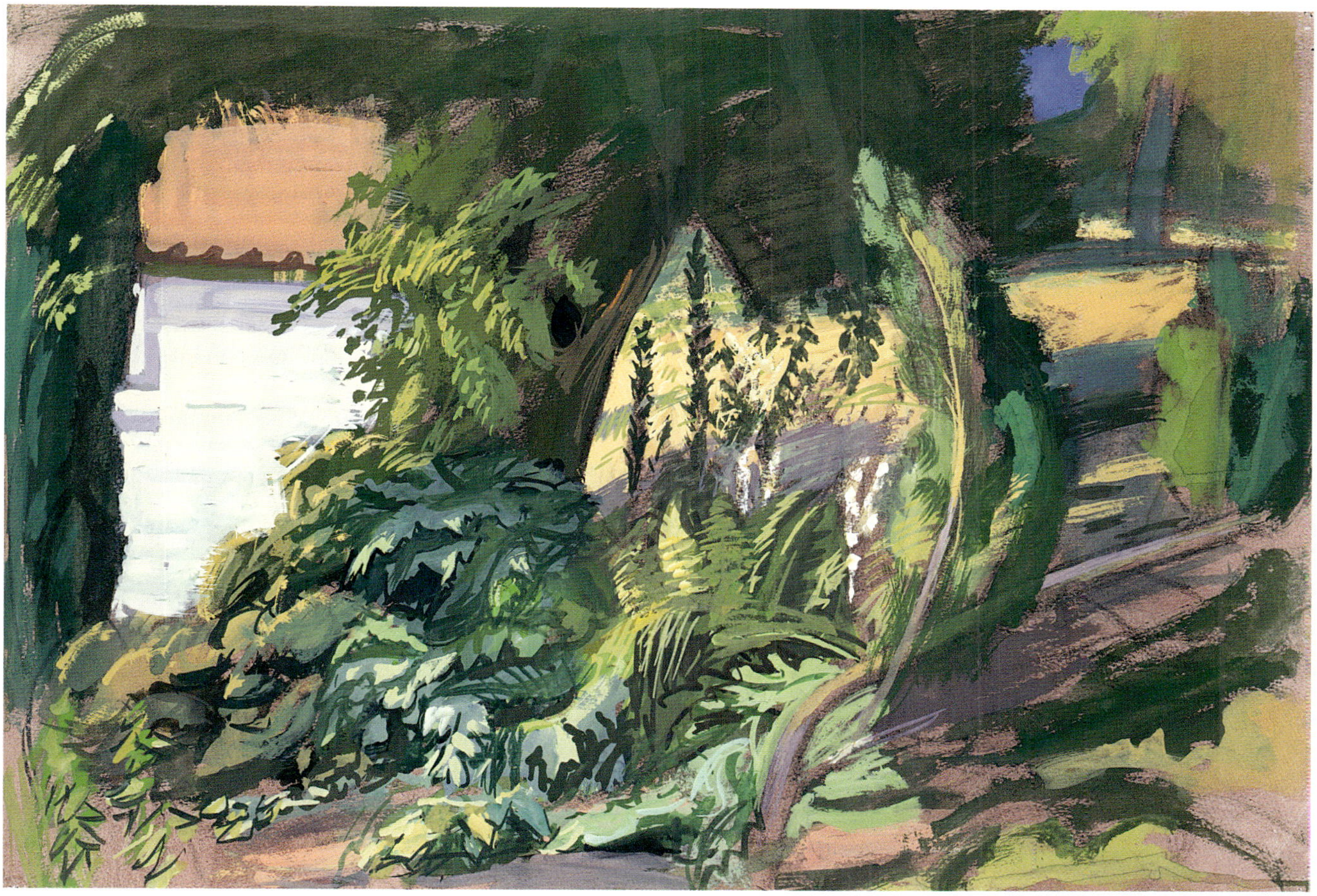

Plate 15
Wye Valley Landscape early 1960s (Cat.76)
Gouache 380 × 540 mm

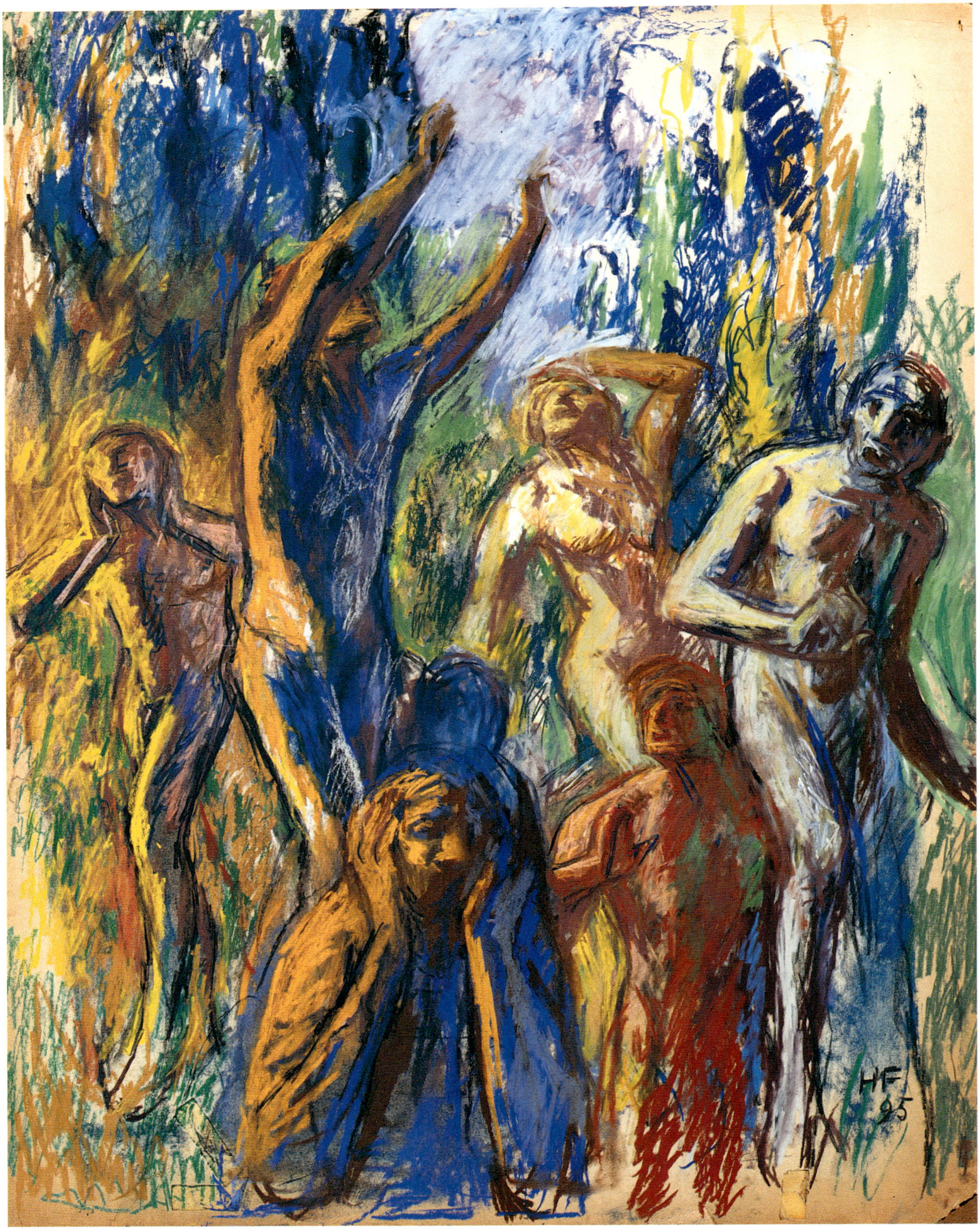

Plate 16
Dream Subject 1995 (Cat.85)
Pastel on card 772 × 566 mm

Exhibition Catalogue

I The Thirties

1 Portrait study for *The Fishmonger (Der Fischhändler)* *c.*1930
Pencil 223 × 150
A sketch for the painting for which Feibusch was awarded the Grand State Prize for Painters by the Prussian Academy of Arts in Berlin.

2 *Power* 1933
Chalk on blue paper 630×480
Signed *HF* and dated

3 *Dancer* 1934
Chalk and pastel on blue paper 775×330
Signed *HF* and dated

4 *The Magician* 1934
Chalk and pastel on blue paper 680×380
Signed *HF* and dated
Colour plate 1

5 *Latona and the Frogs* 1934
Chalk and pastel 655×495
Signed *HF* and dated
Colour plate 3

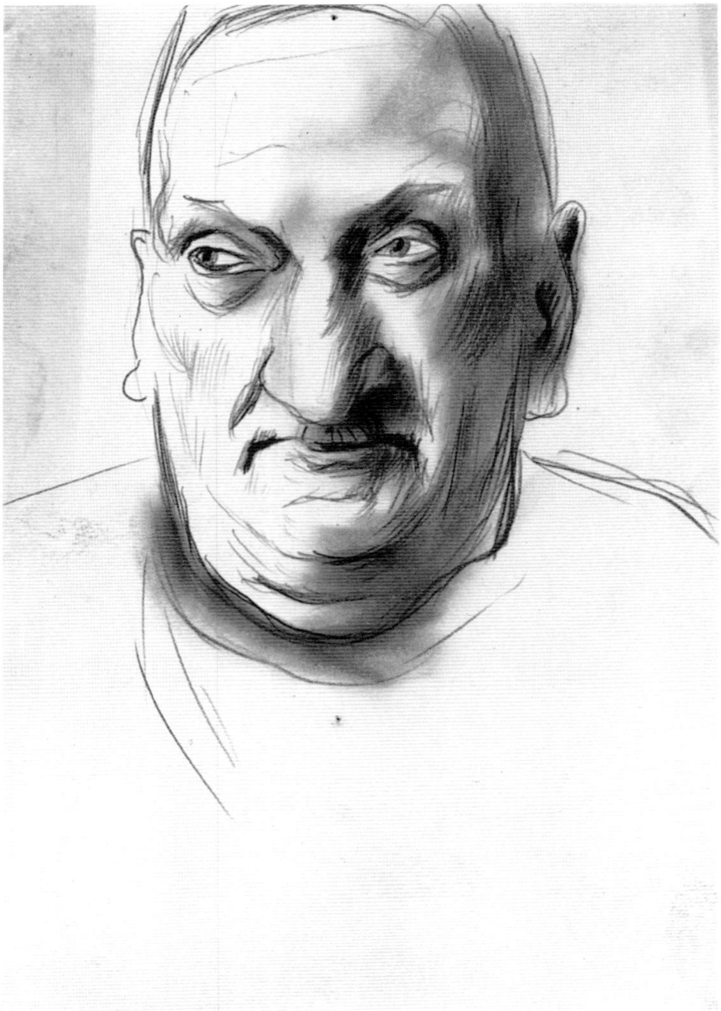

1

All measurements are given in millimetres, height before width.
All works belong to private collections.

Subjects not illustrated in the Catalogue section can be found in the Colour plates between pages 33 and 48.

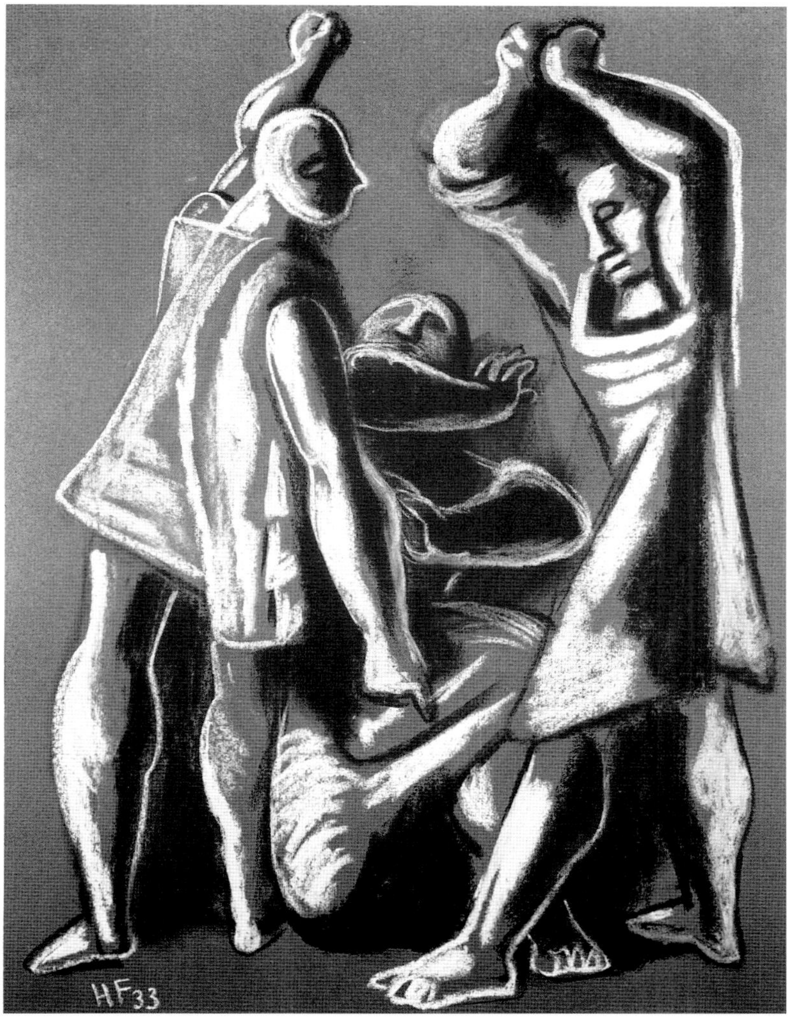

2

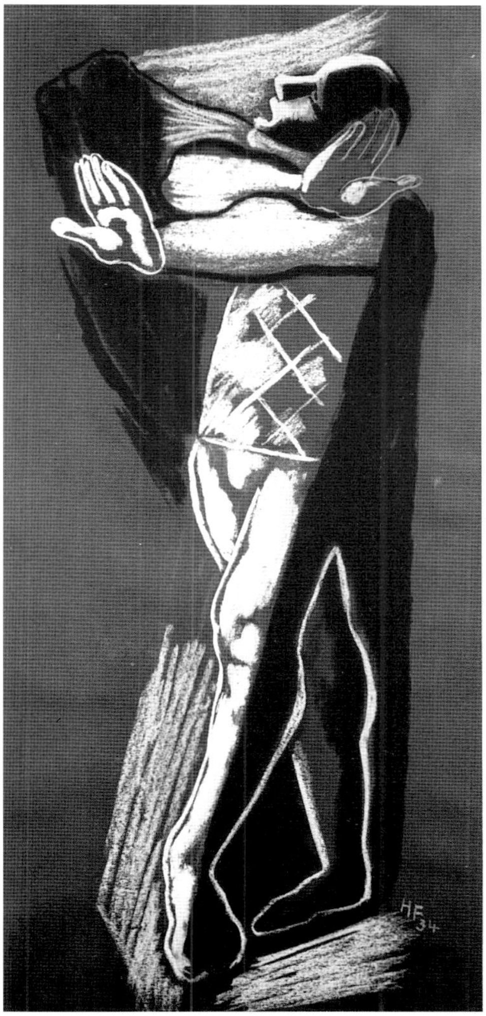

3

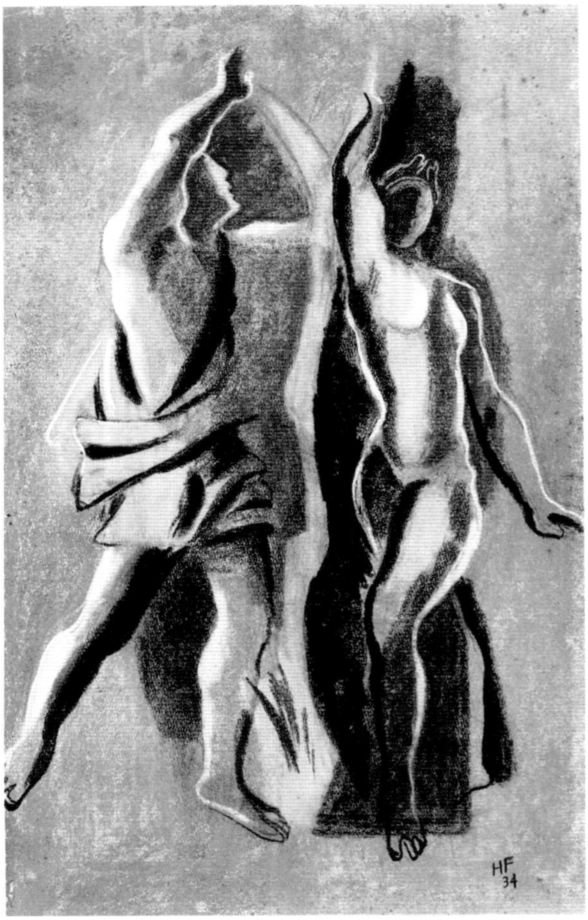

6

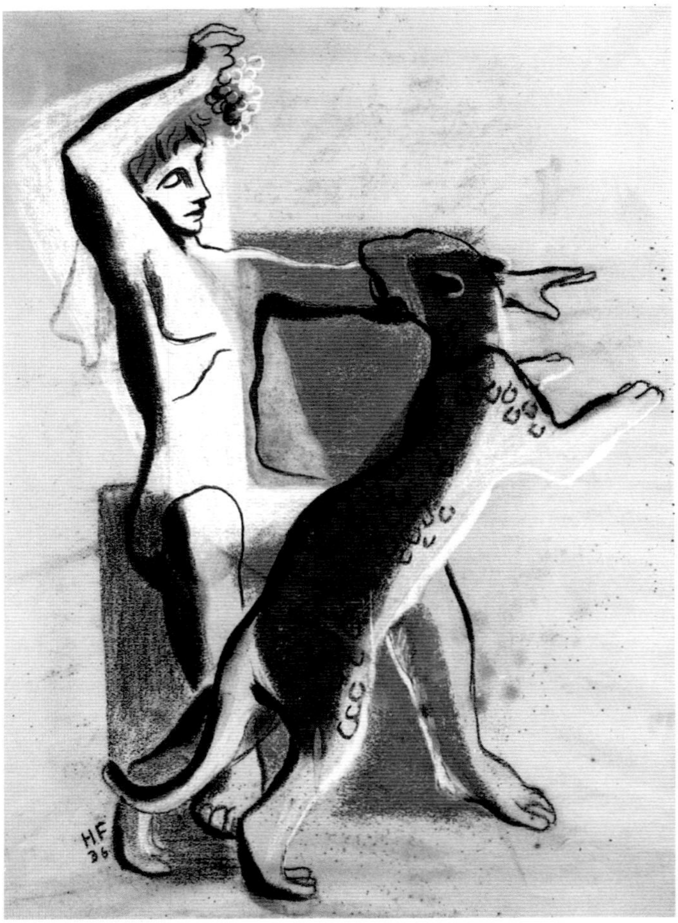

9

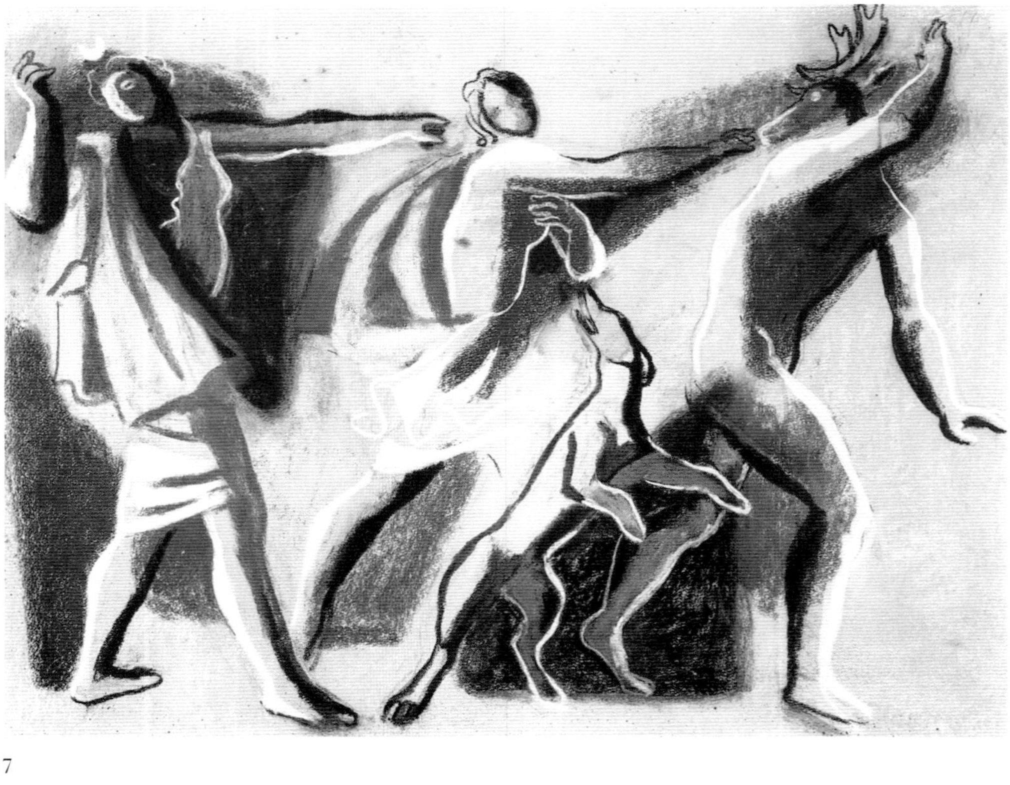
7

6 *Apollo and Daphne* 1934
Chalk and pastel 665×410
Signed *HF* and dated

7 *Diana and Actaeon* *c.*1934
Chalk and pastel 505×665

8 *A Group of Apes* 1935
Chalk and pastel 460×630
Signed *HF* and dated
Colour plate 2

9 *Apollo and a Leopard* 1936
Chalk and pastel 660×510
Signed *HF* and dated

10 *Seated Draped Figure* 1937
Charcoal 680×380
Signed *HF* and dated

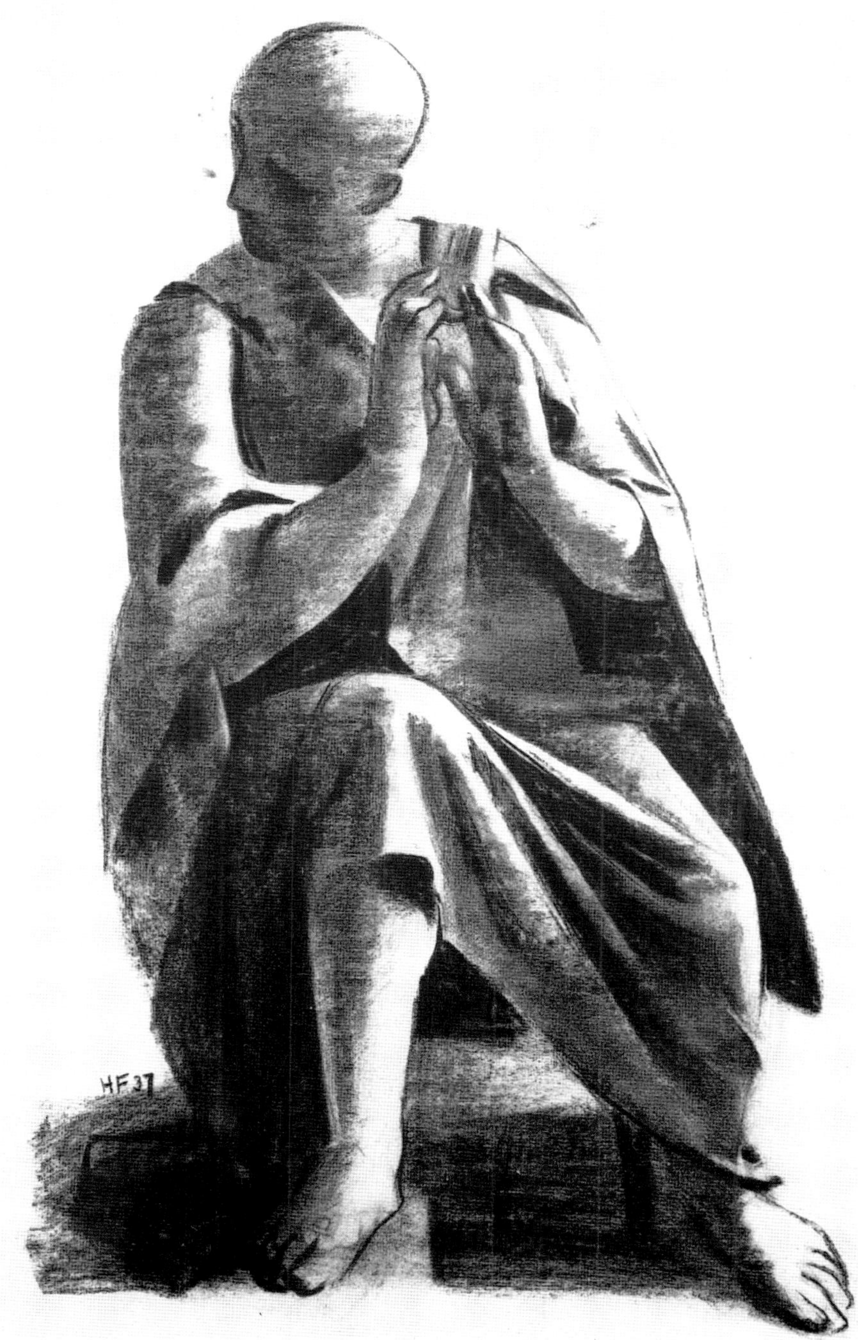

10

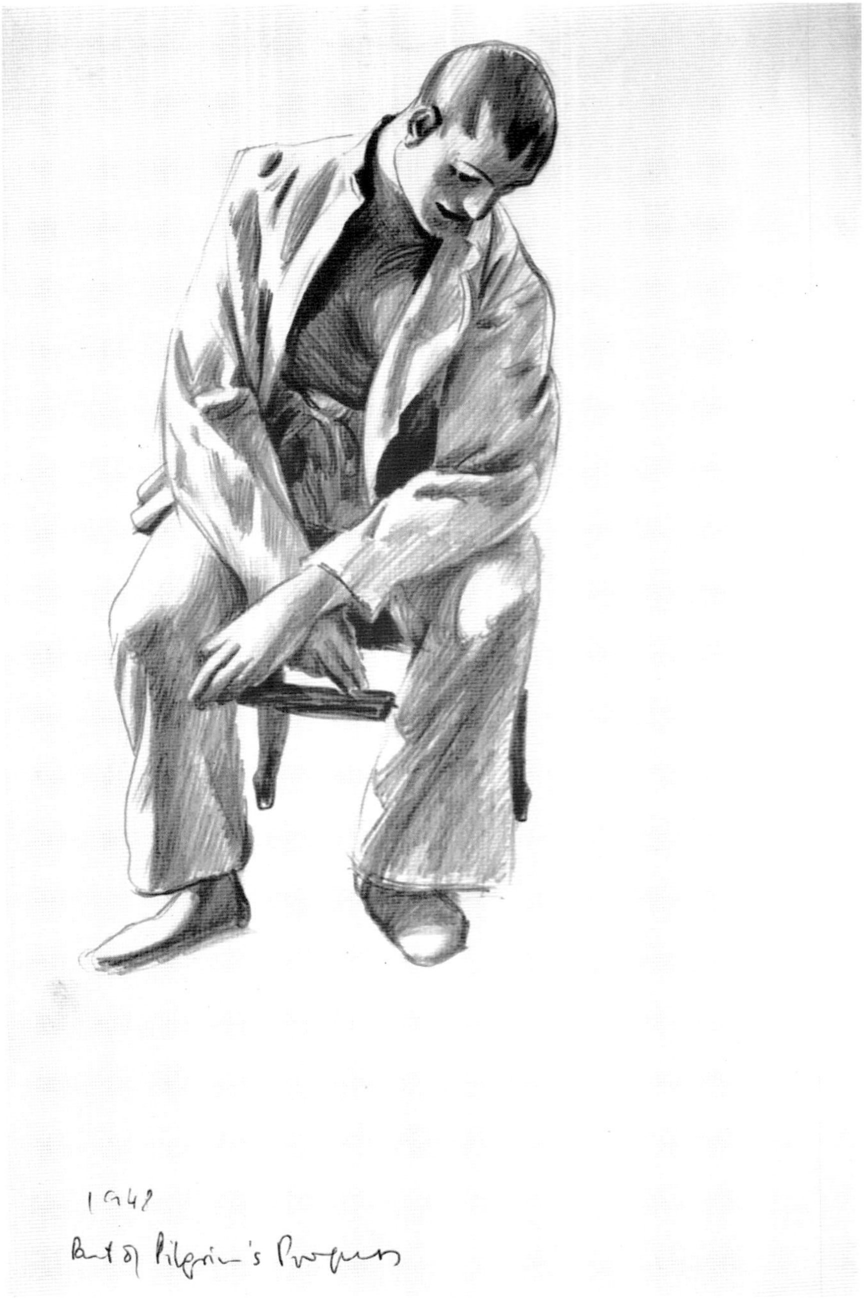

11

11 *Seated Male Figure c.*1937
Pencil 355×230
Incorrectly inscribed *1948. Part of Pilgrim's Progress*

12 *Elijah c.*1937
Charcoal and pastel on green paper 630×480
Closely related to a lithograph of the same subject.

13 *A Circus of Sea Creatures* 1938
Gouache on card 192×570
Signed *HF* and dated
Sketch for a mural in Petworth Cottage, Bosham, Sussex.

14 *1939* 1939
Oil on board 1530×915
Signed *HF* and dated

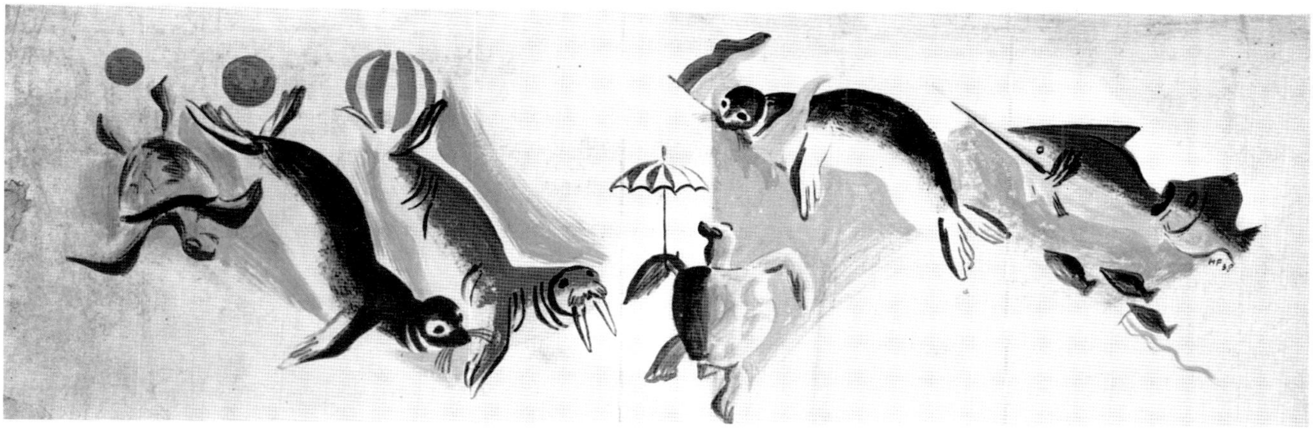

13

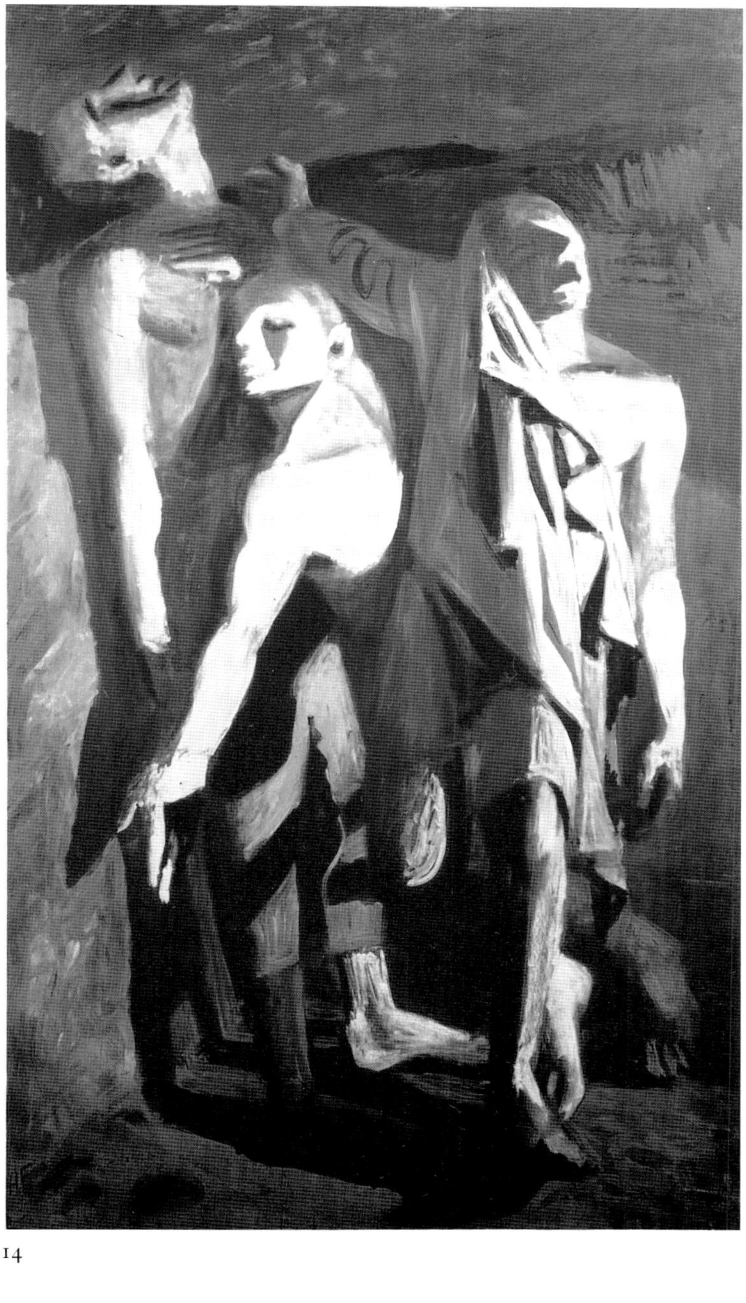

14

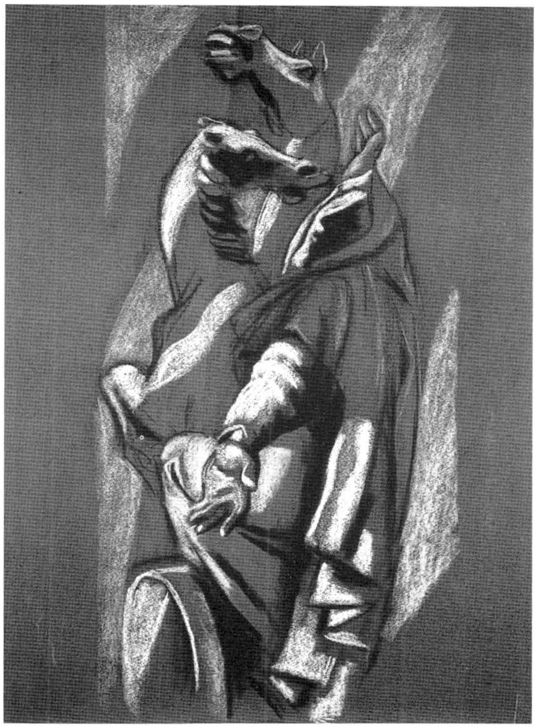

12

II The Artist and His Family

15 *Portrait of the Artist's Grandmother*
1931
Pencil 304×291
Signed *HF* and dated

16 *Self Portrait, Head and Shoulders*
1932
Ink and black chalk 285×230
Signed *HF* and dated

17 *The Artist's Mother and Wife* (n.d.)
Chalk and conté 460×615

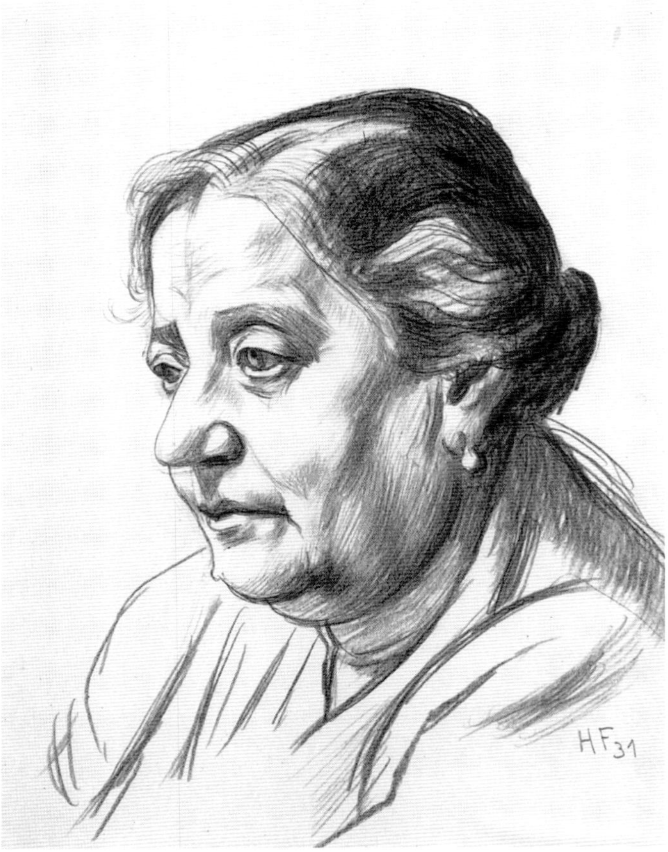

15

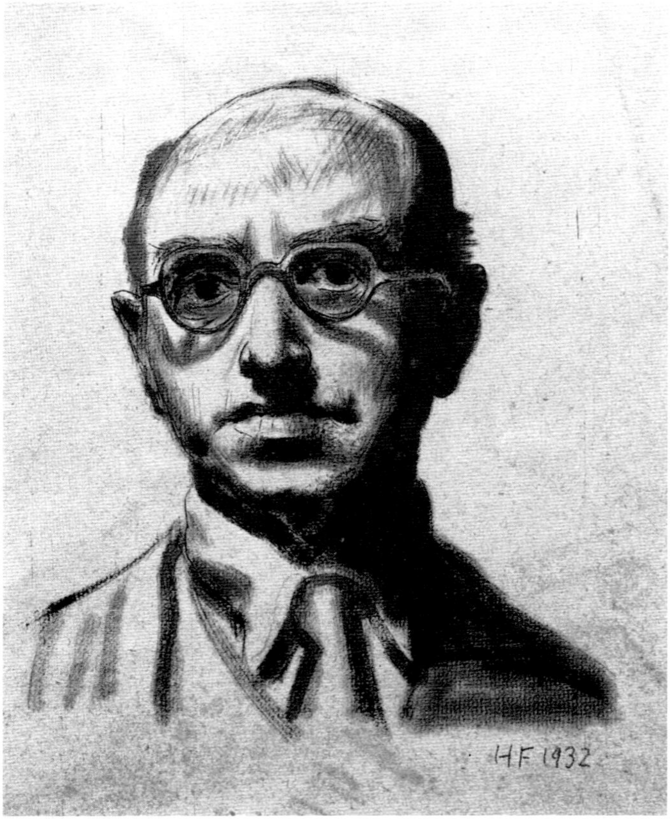

16

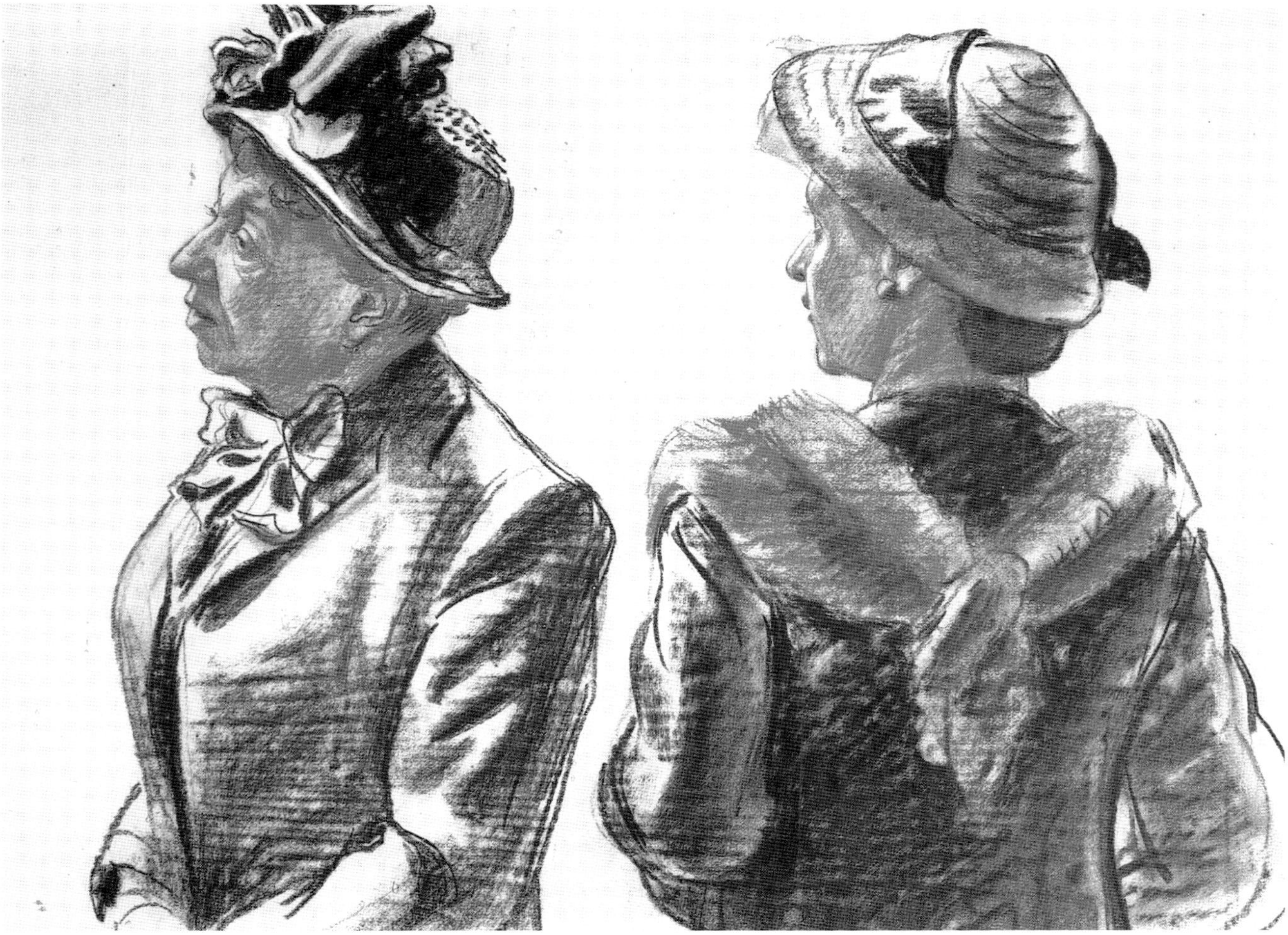

17

III Animals

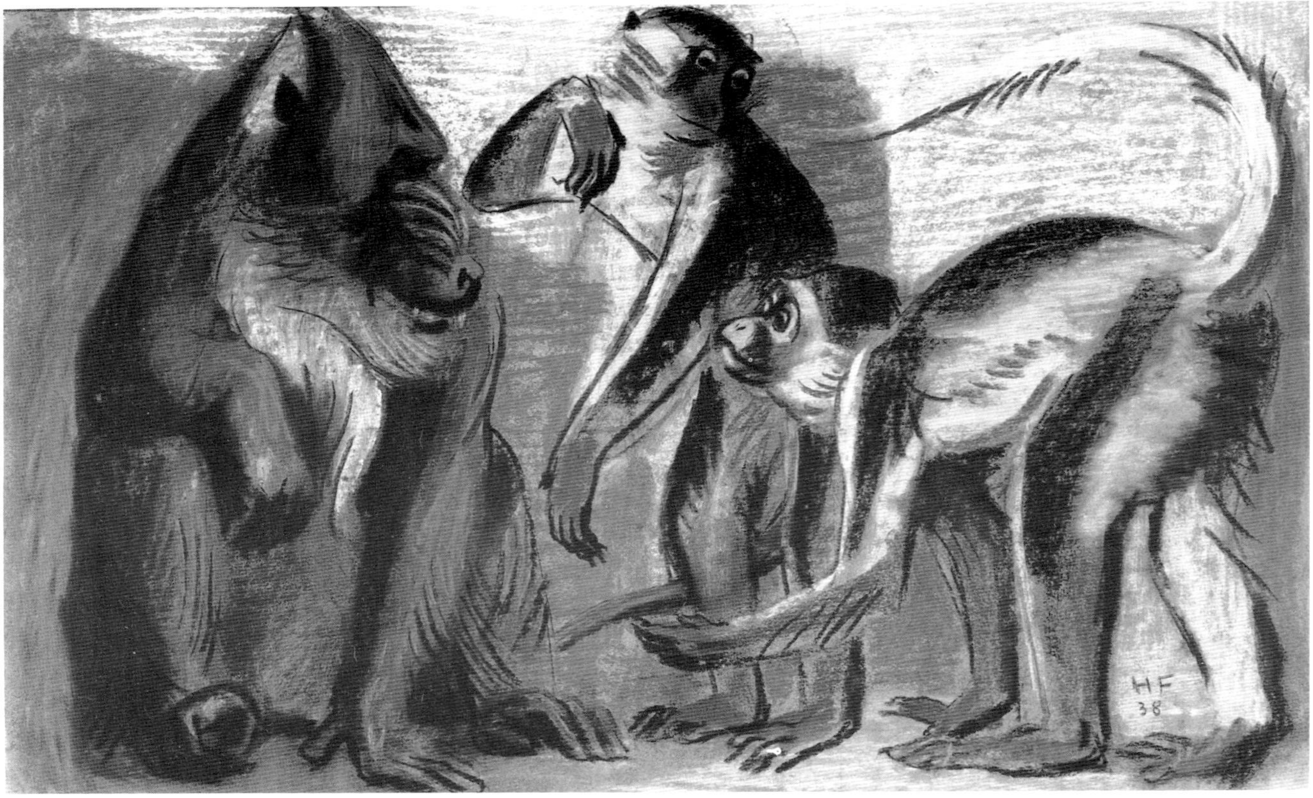

18

All of Feibusch's work in which animals form the main subject appear to date from the mid to late 1930s.

18 *Mandrill and Mangabeys* 1938
Pastel 410×650
Signed *HF* and dated
A sketch for the lithograph produced by Feibusch as his contribution to the 'School Prints' series, twenty-four lithographs produced by British artists during 1946-7 for display in schools.

19 *Study of a Seated Mandrill* (n.d.)
Pencil and chalk 220×150

20 *Study of a Mandrill* (n.d.)
Pencil and black chalk 164×140

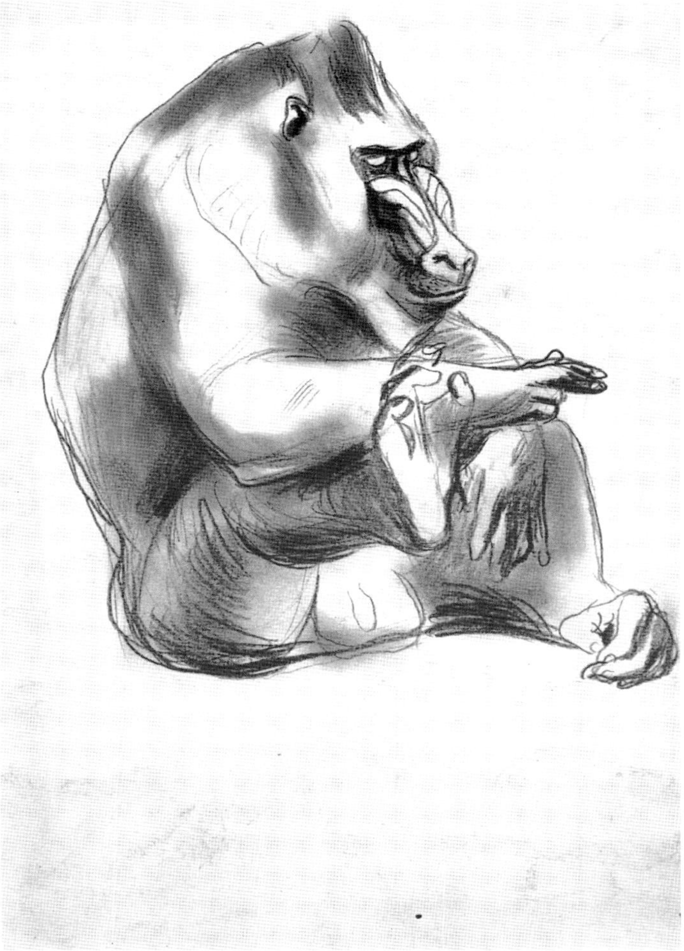

19

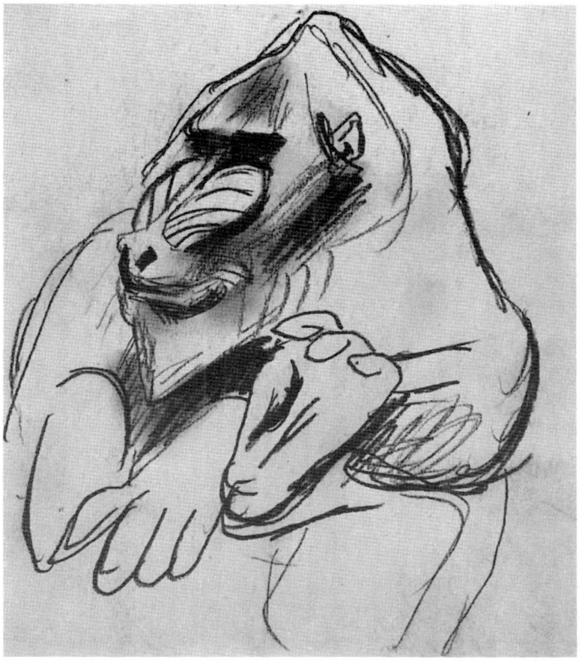

20

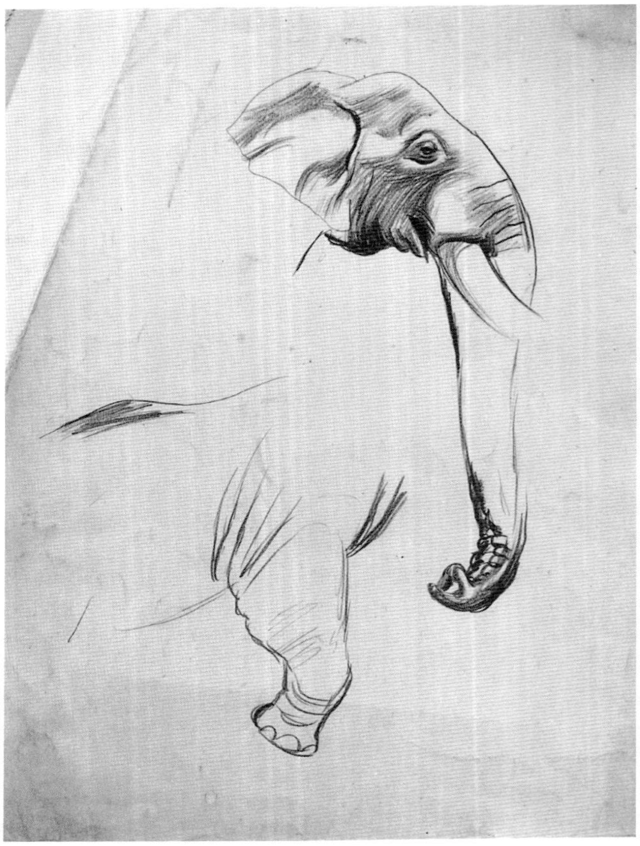

22

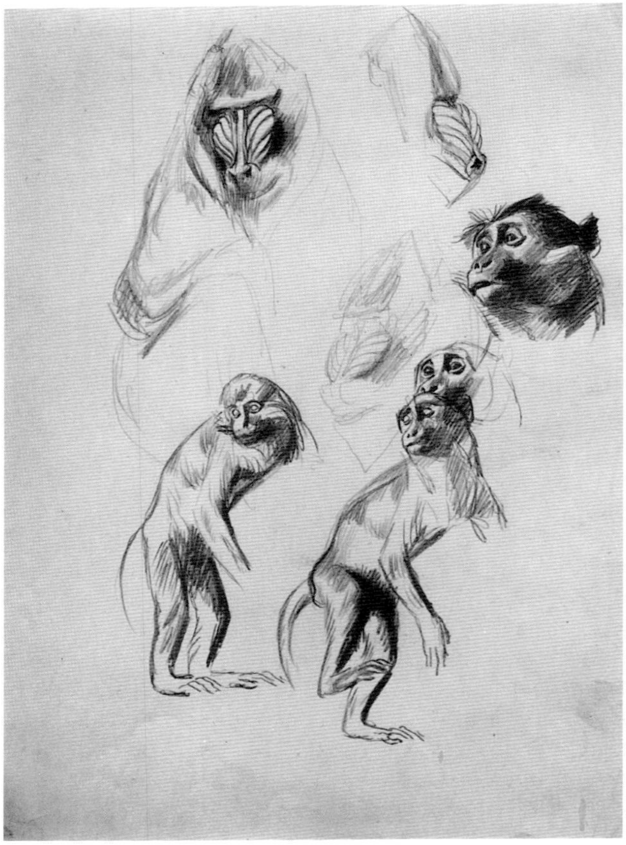

21

21 *Mandrills and Monkeys* (n.d.)
Pencil 280×203

22 *Studies of an Elephant* (n.d.)
Pencil 280×206

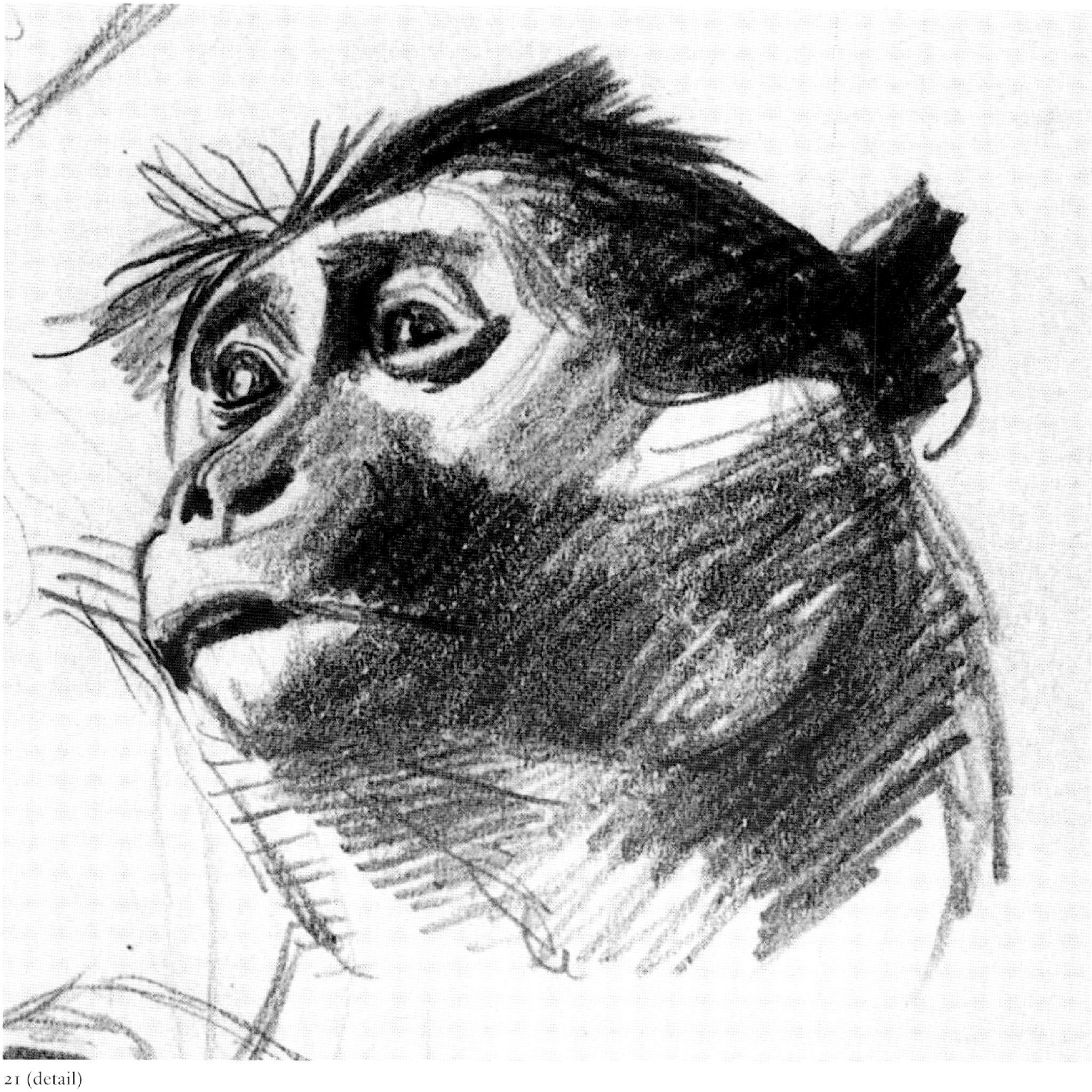
21 (detail)

IV Preparatory Work for Murals and Paintings

M numbers in brackets refer to the list of murals which can be found on p.24.

23 Sketch for *Footwashing* 1938 (M1)
Methodist Chapel, Colliers Wood, London SW19
Pencil 176×230

24 Sketch for *Footwashing* 1938 (M1)
See Cat.23
Pastel 180×240
Signed *HF* and dated
Inscribed *for Paul from Hans*

25 Sketch for *Nativity* 1940 (M2)
Saint Wilfrid's, Elm Grove, Brighton
Gouache on card 350×1015
Signed *HF* and dated

26 Study for a naked figure of Christian, for *Pilgrim's Progress* *c.*1944 (M4)
Saint Elisabeth's, Victoria Drive, Eastbourne, Sussex
Pencil 355×232

27 Study for a standing female figure holding a cloth for *Pilgrim's Progress* *c.*1944 (M4)
See Cat.26
Charcoal, chalk and conté 480×320
Wrongly inscribed *Study for Mural* c.*1950*

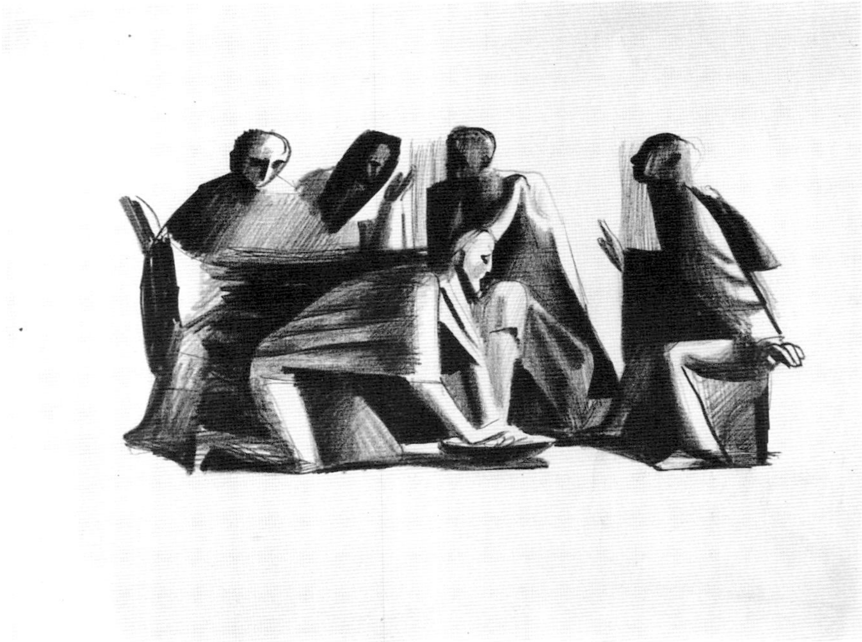

23

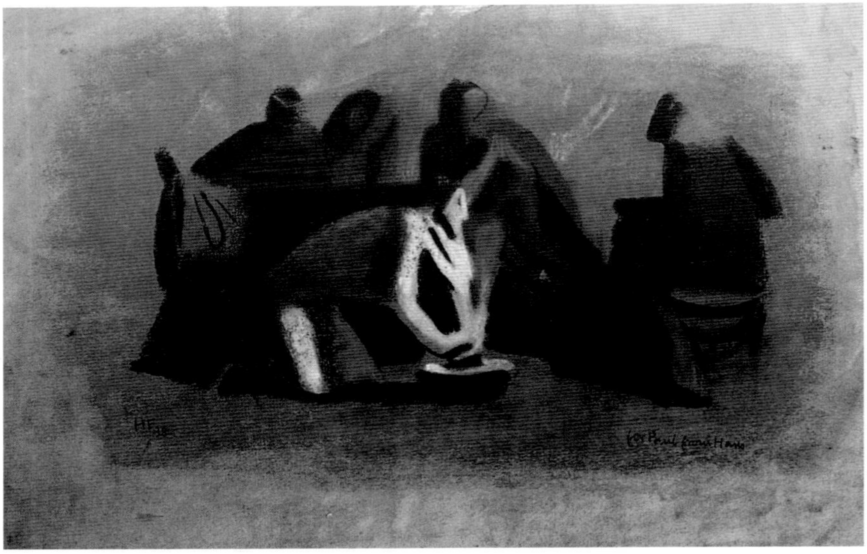

24

To stand in front of an empty wall, to see, as it were, into it and visualise shapes and colours moving towards the surface, gave me the most intense feeling of life and joy.

Hans Feibusch in *Hans Feibusch: An Eightieth Birthday Exhibition*, Greater London Council exh.cat., 1978

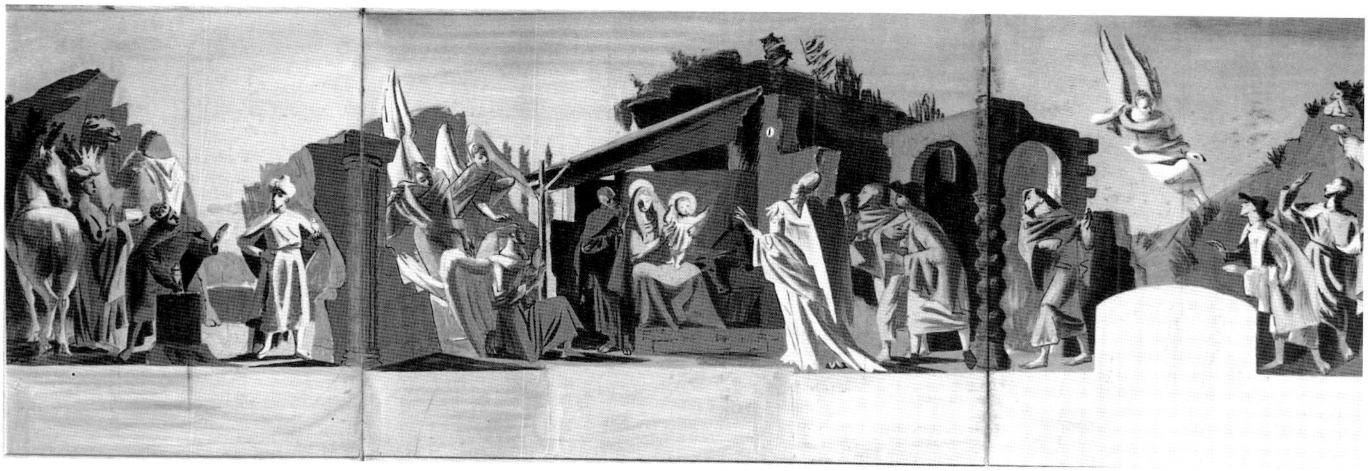

25

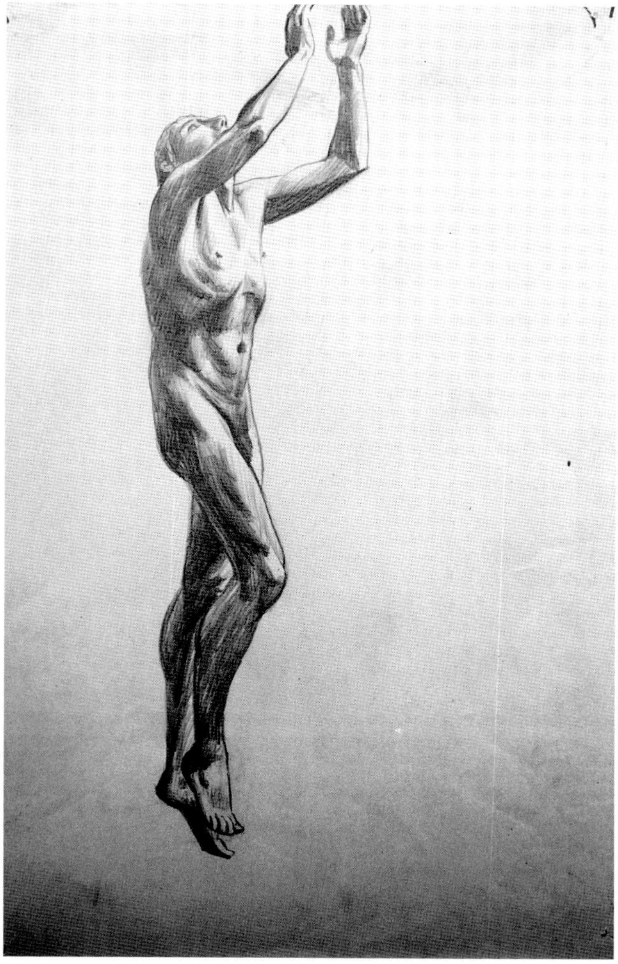

26

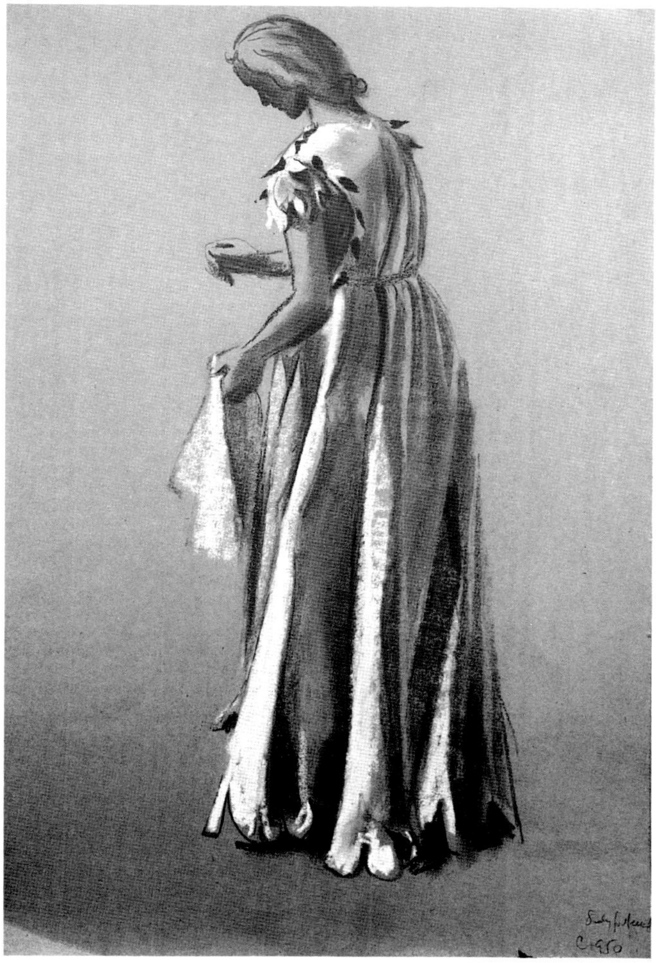

27

28 Study for a running figure of Christiana for *Pilgrim's Progress* *c.*1944 (M4)
See Cat.26
Charcoal, chalk and conté 480×320

29 Sketch for *The Return of the Prodigal Son* 1950 (M8)
All Saints, Iden, Sussex
Gouache 510×710
Signed *HF* and dated

30 Study for the two figures in *Baptism of Christ* *c.*1950 (M9)
The Cathedral of the Holy Trinity, Chichester, Sussex
Chalk and conté on grey paper 575×420

31 Sketch for *Baptism of Christ* *c.*1950 (M9)
See Cat.30
Pastel on grey paper 752×550

32 Sketch for *Baptism of Christ* 1950 (M9)
See Cat.30
Ink and gouache 763×547
Signed *HF* and dated

33 Sketch for *Baptism of Christ* 1950–1 (M9)
See Cat.30
Gouache 710×410
Signed *HF*
Colour plate 4

34 Sketch for an unidentified mural *Scenes from the Life of Christ* 1952
Gouache 454×373
Signed *HF* and dated
Colour plate 5

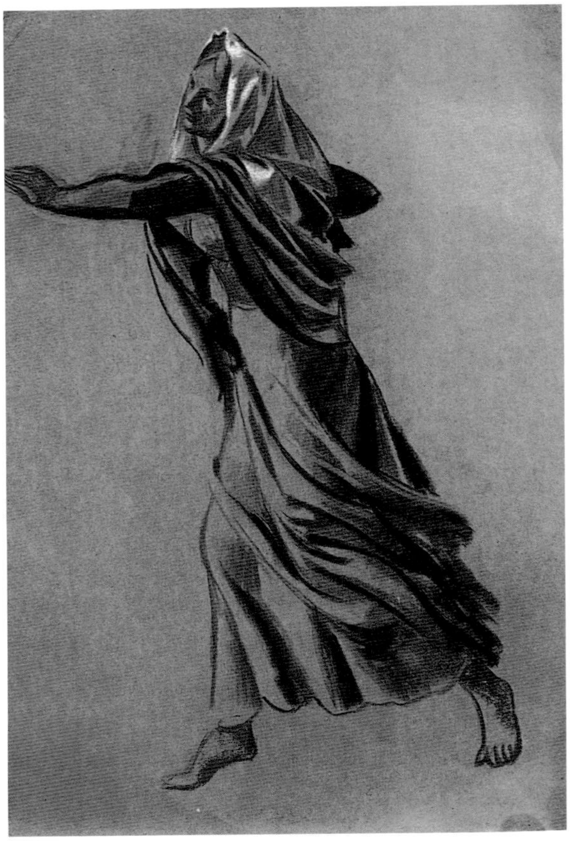

28

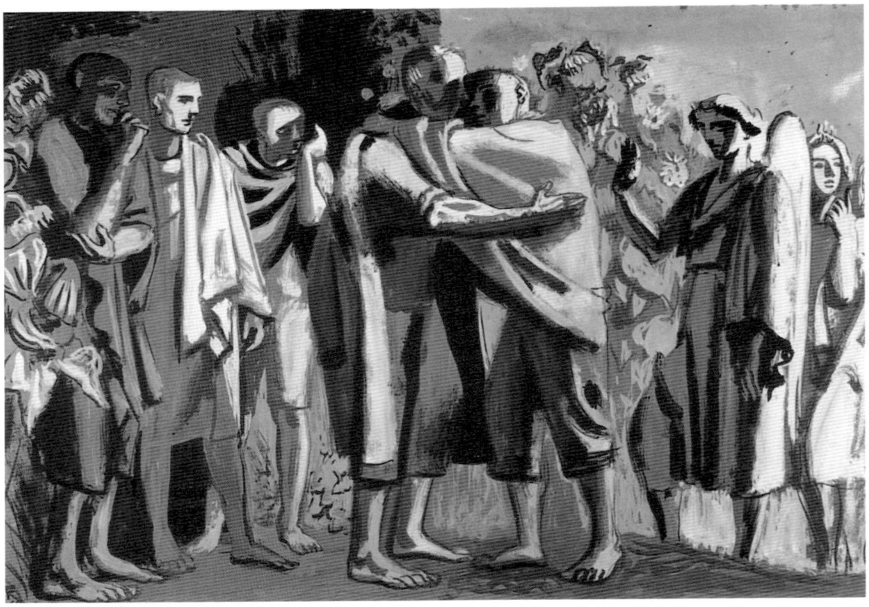

29

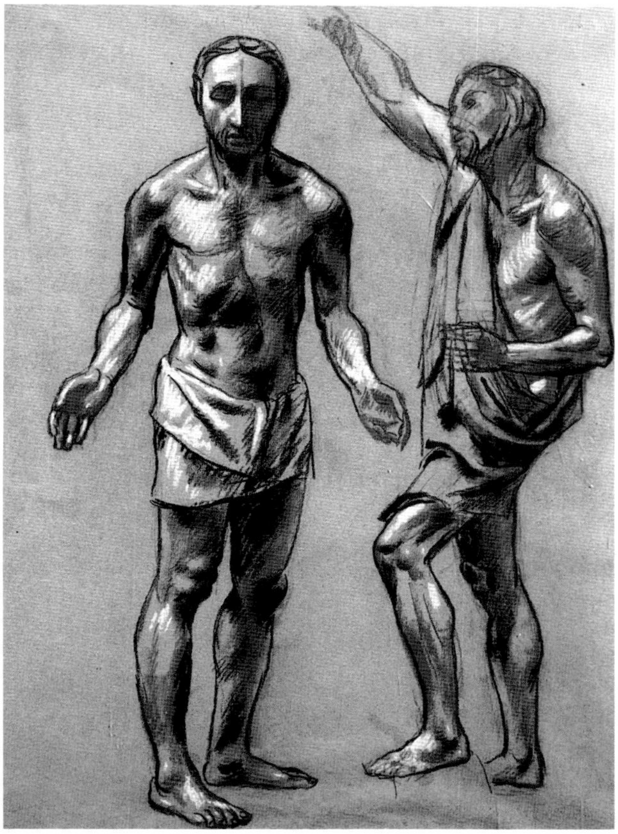

30

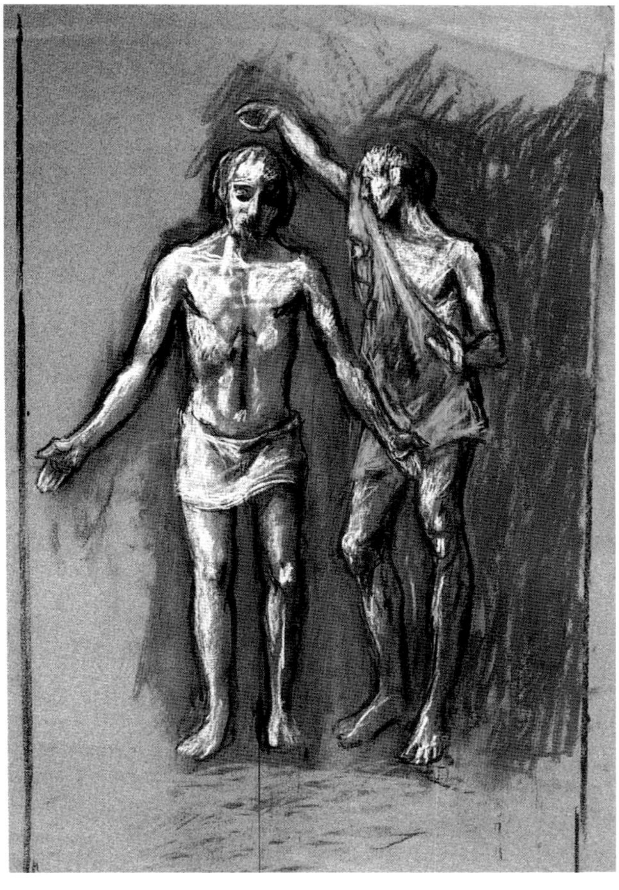

31

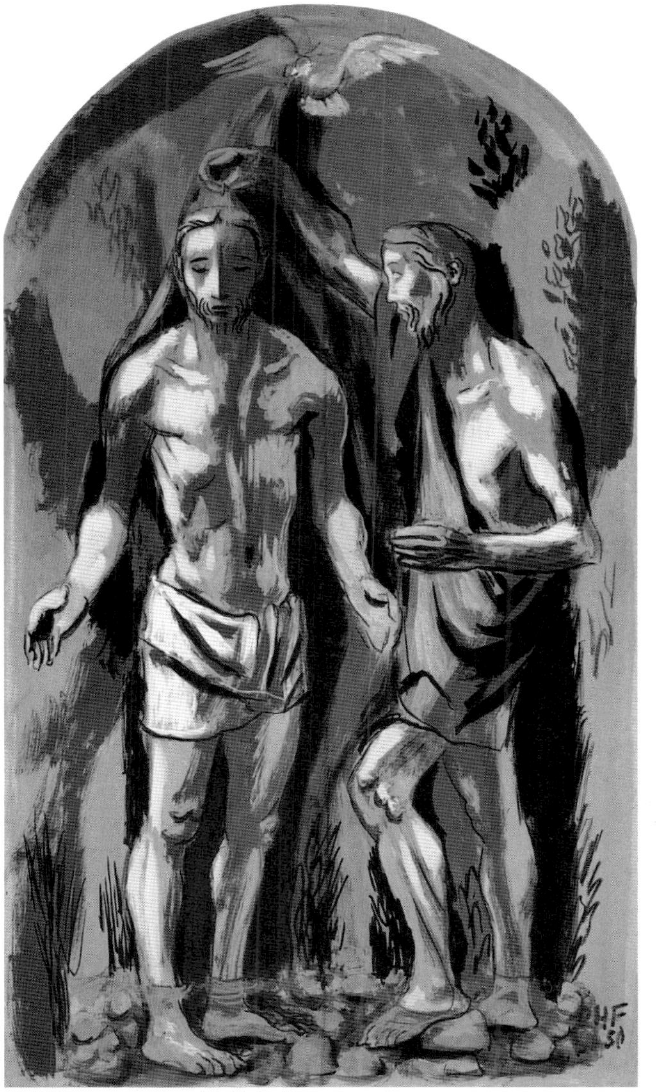

32

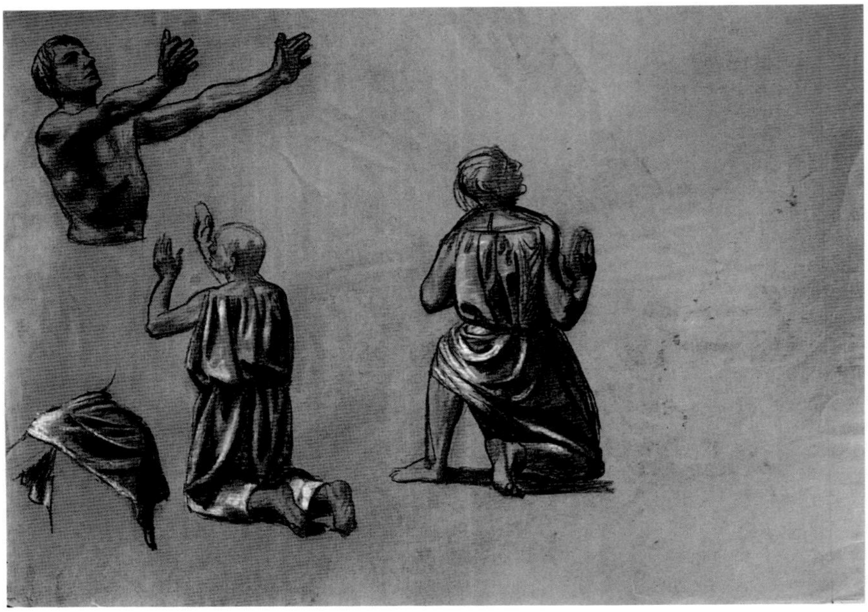

36

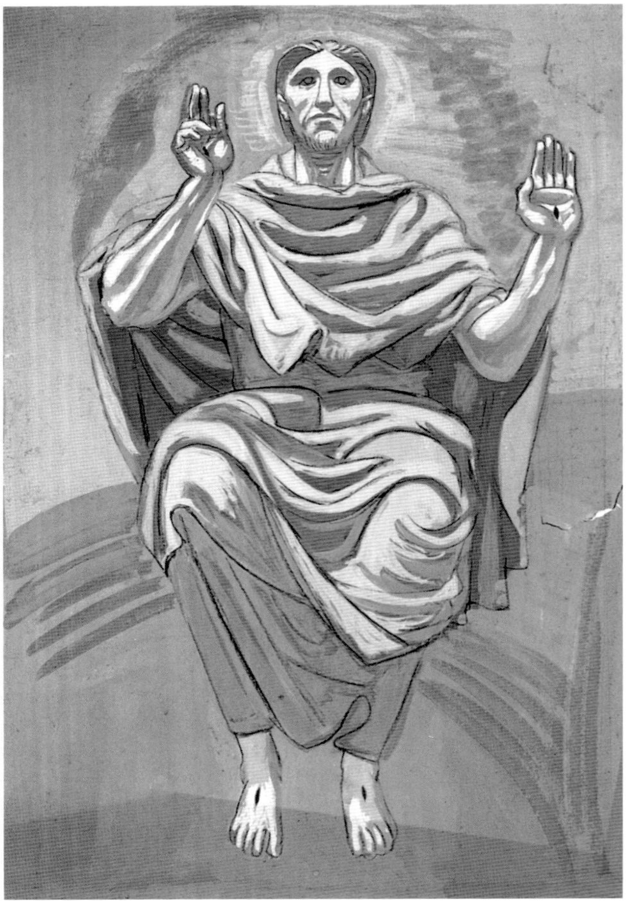

35

35 Study for the figure of Christ for *Christ in Majesty c.*1954 (M14)
Saint Mary's, Goring-by-Sea, Sussex
Gouache on card 816×560

36 Figure and drapery studies for *Ascension c.*1955 (M15)
Saint Mary's, Grove Road, Welling, Kent
Charcoal, chalk and conté 480×645

37 Sketch for the *Resurrection Triptych* 1956-7 (M20)
Saint James's, Martin Way, Merton, London SW20
Gouache 350×570
Exh: *Jewish Artists of Great Britain* at Cartwright Hall, Bradford, 1978

38 Early sketch for the mural at Saint Peter's, Pickford Lane, Bexleyheath, Kent *c.*1956-7 (M22)
Gouache 255×340

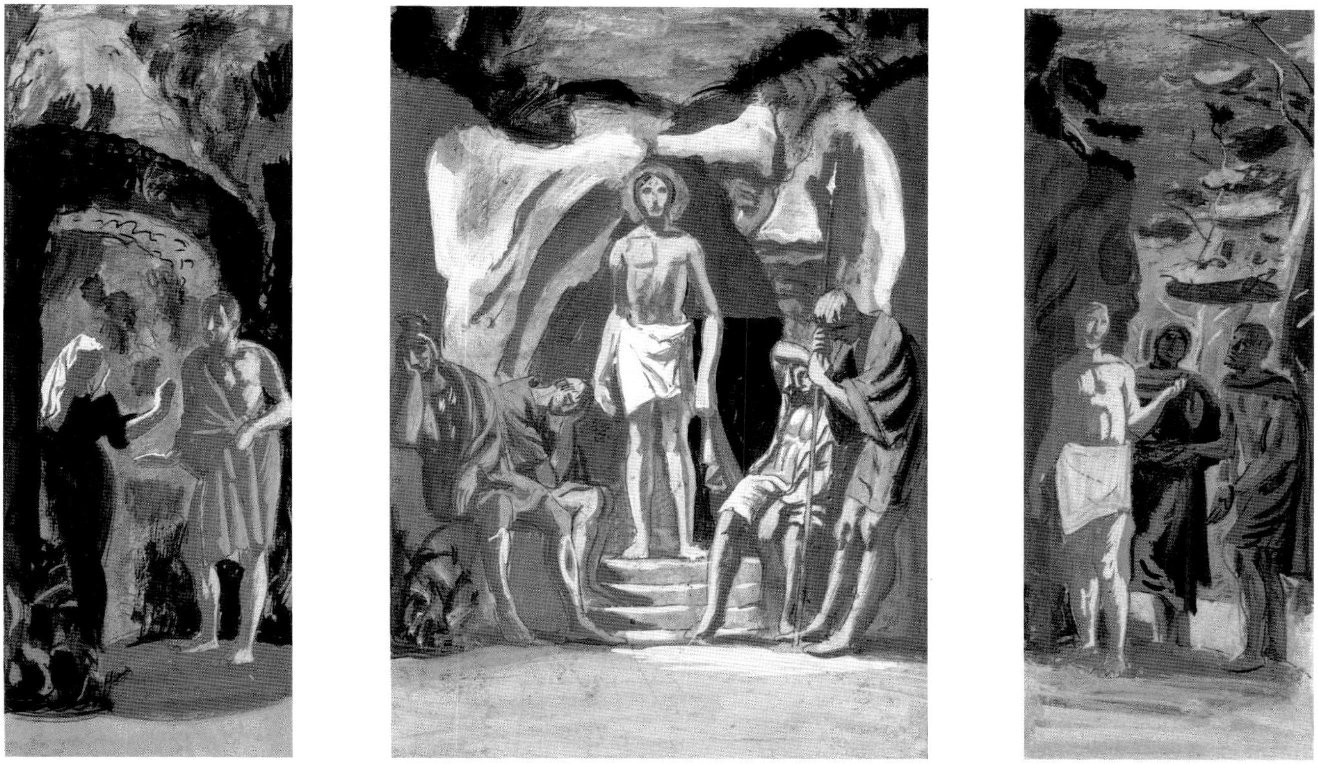

37

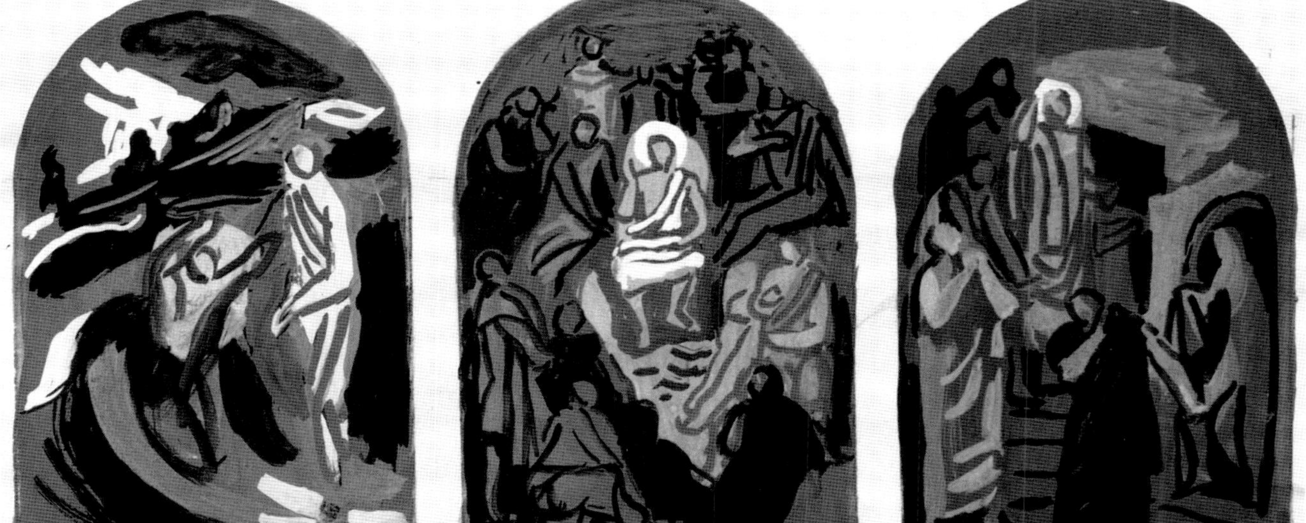

38

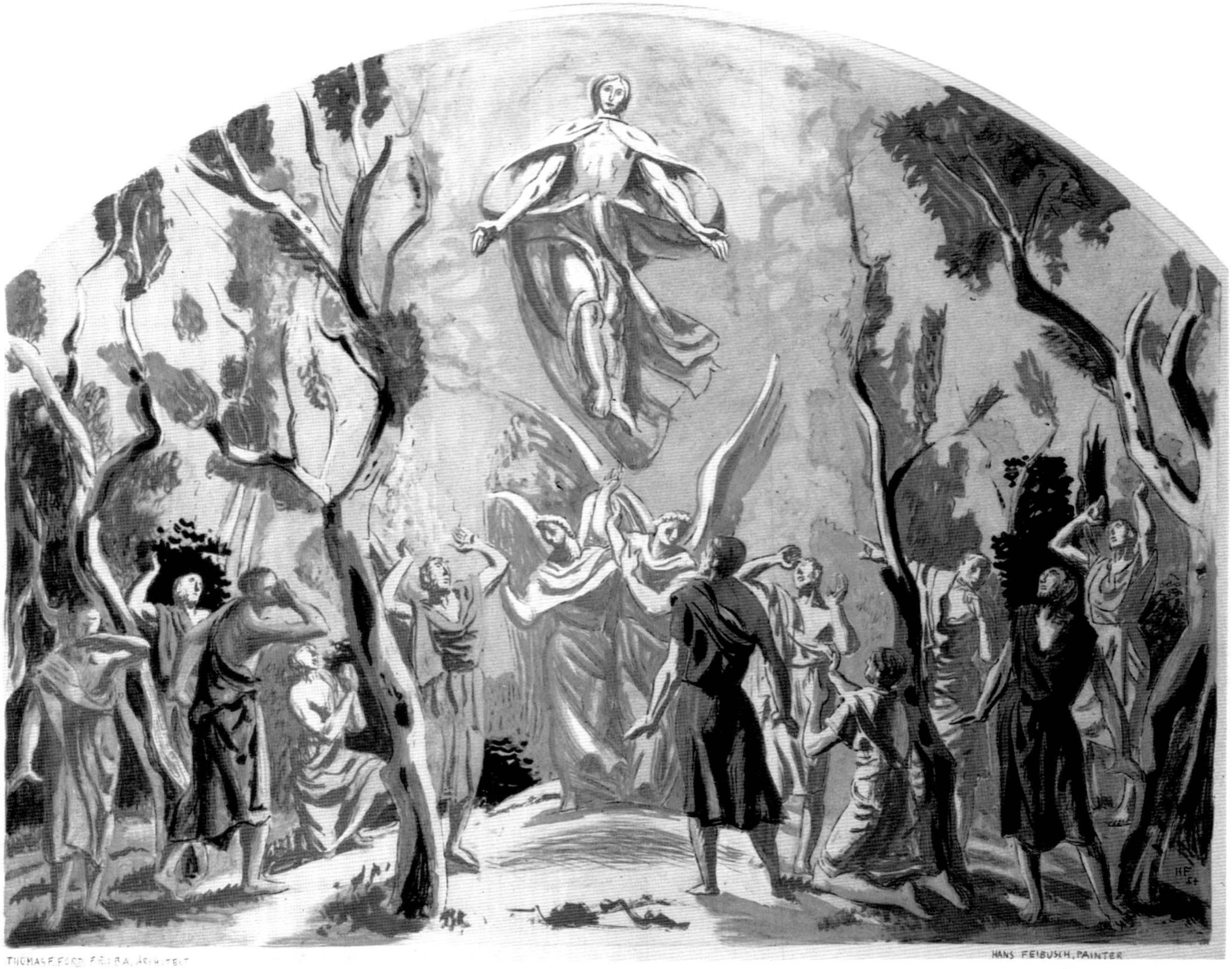

40

39 Study for the figure of the Risen Christ for *Ascension c.*1957 (M21)
All Saints, Herbert Road, Plumstead, London SE18
Charcoal, chalk and conté 630×480

40 Sketch for *Ascension c.*1957 (M21)
See Cat.39
Gouache 467×583
Inscribed *Thomas F. Ford FRIBA, Architect*
Hans Feibusch, Painter

41 Sketch for *Christ in Glory* 1957 (M26)
Saint Sidwell's, Sidwell Street, Exeter, Devon
Gouache on card 553×492
Signed *HF* and dated

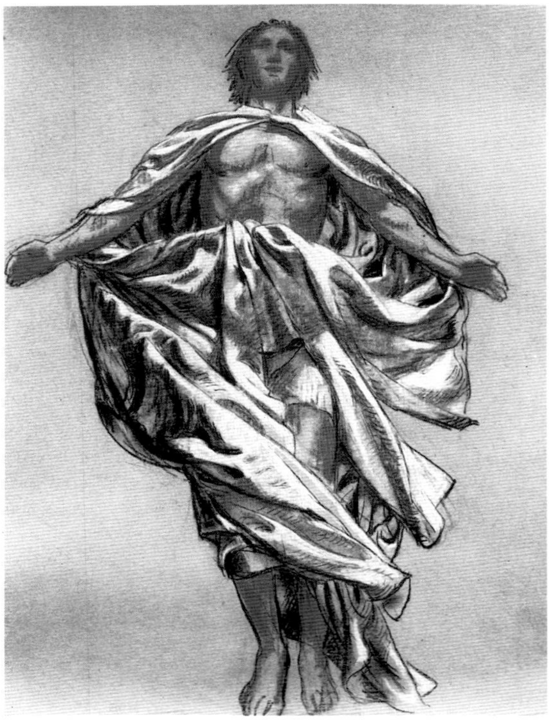

39

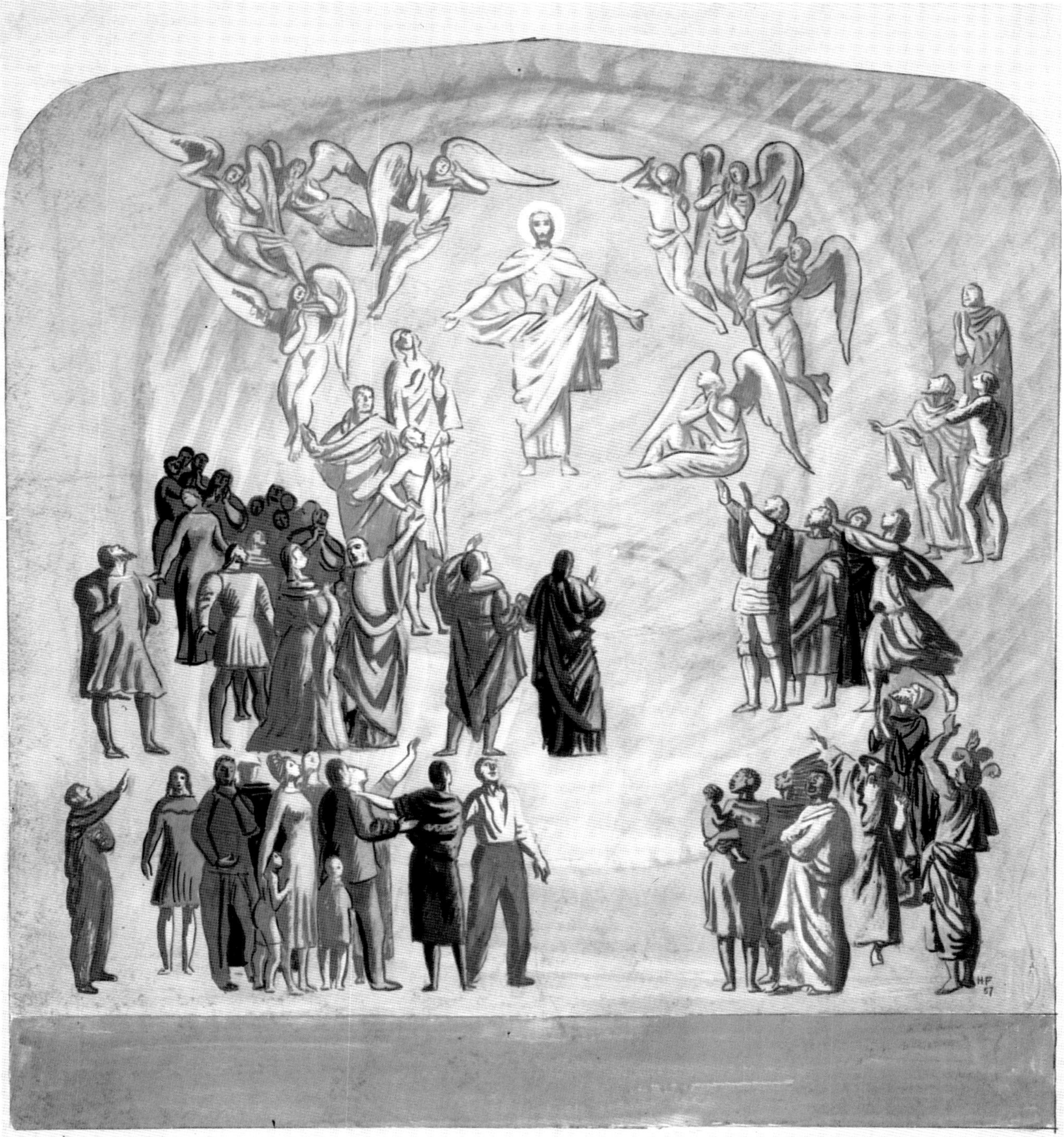

41

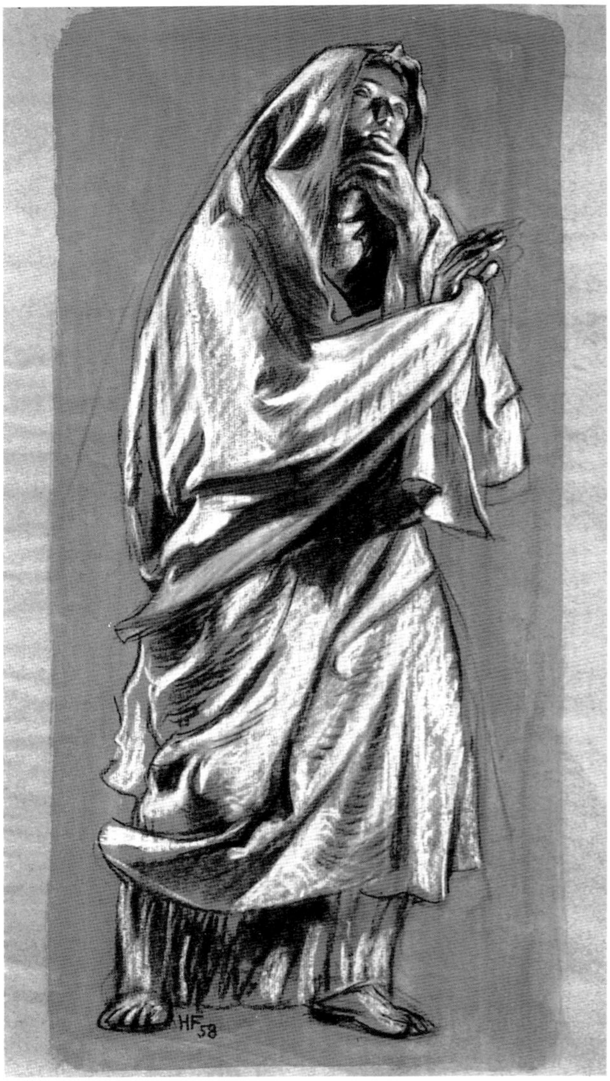

43

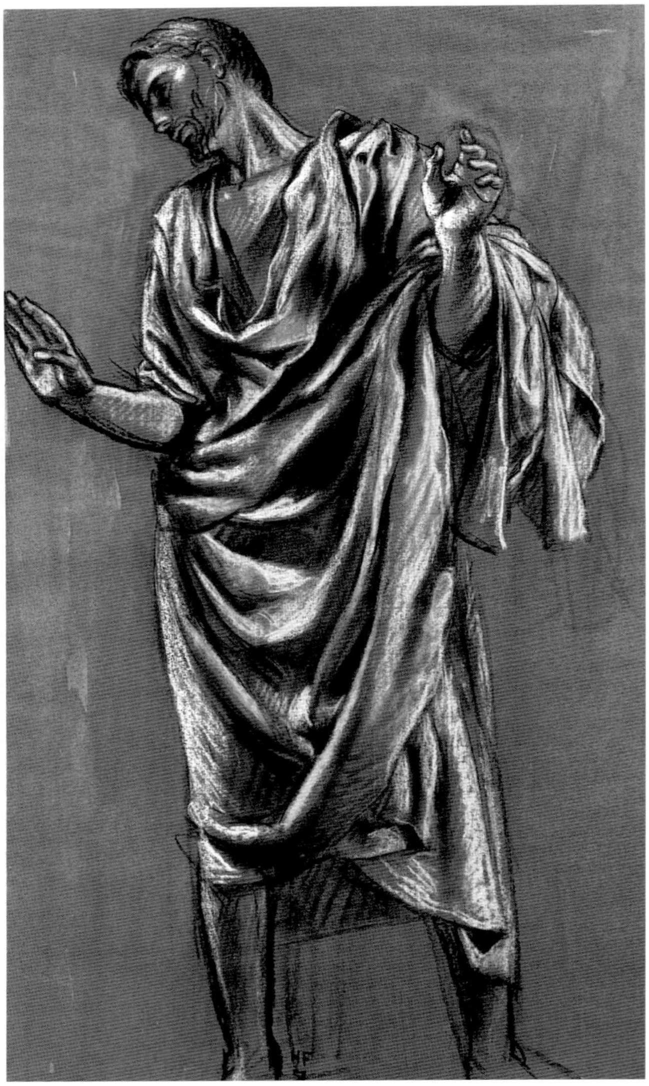

42

42 Study for the figure of Christ for *Noli Me Tangere* 1957 (M25)
All Hallows, Union Street, Southwark, London SE1
Chalk and wash 565×355
Signed *HF* and dated

43 Study for the figure of Mary Magdalene for *Noli Me Tangere* 1958 (M25)
See Cat.42
Charcoal, pastel and wash 620×480
Signed *HF* and dated

44 Studies for two male standing figures for *Baptism of Christ* 1960 (M31)
Old Saint George's Baptist Church, Catherine Street, Plymouth, Devon
Charcoal, pastel and watercolour 630×485
Signed *HF* and dated

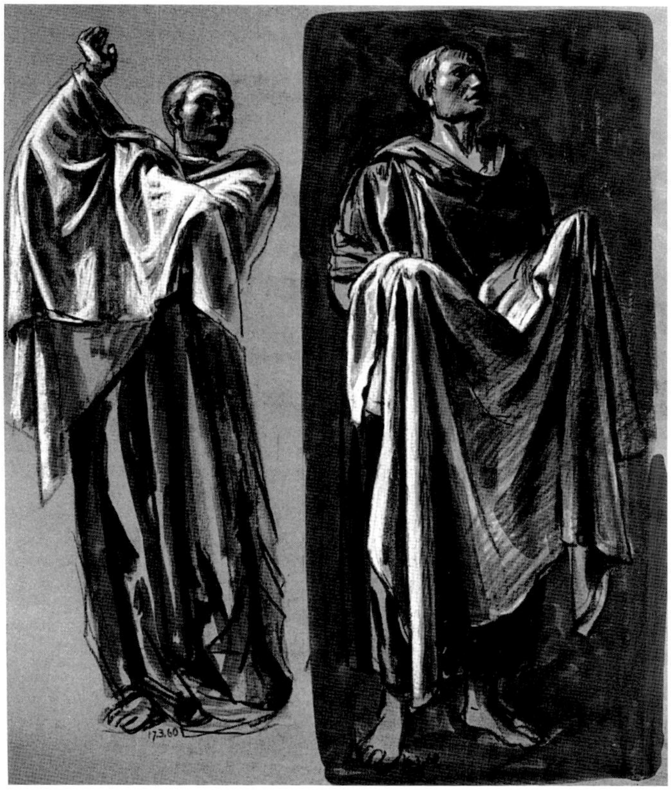

44

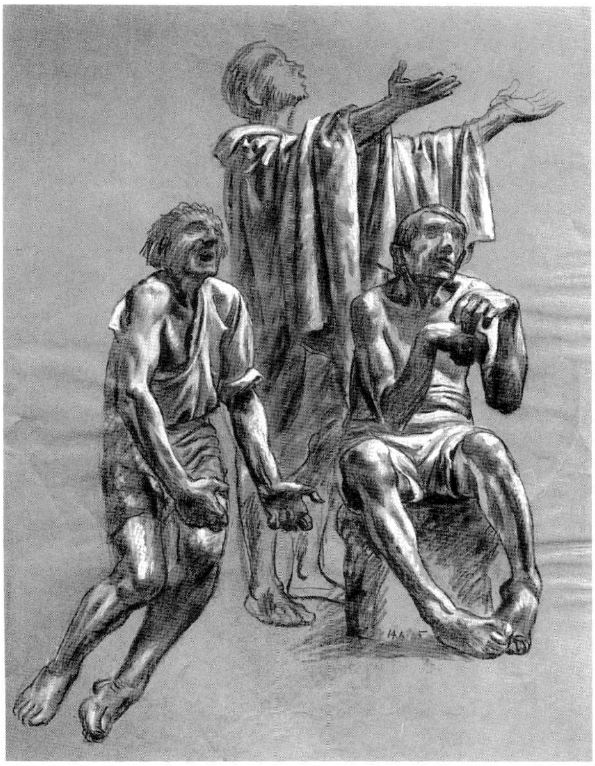

46

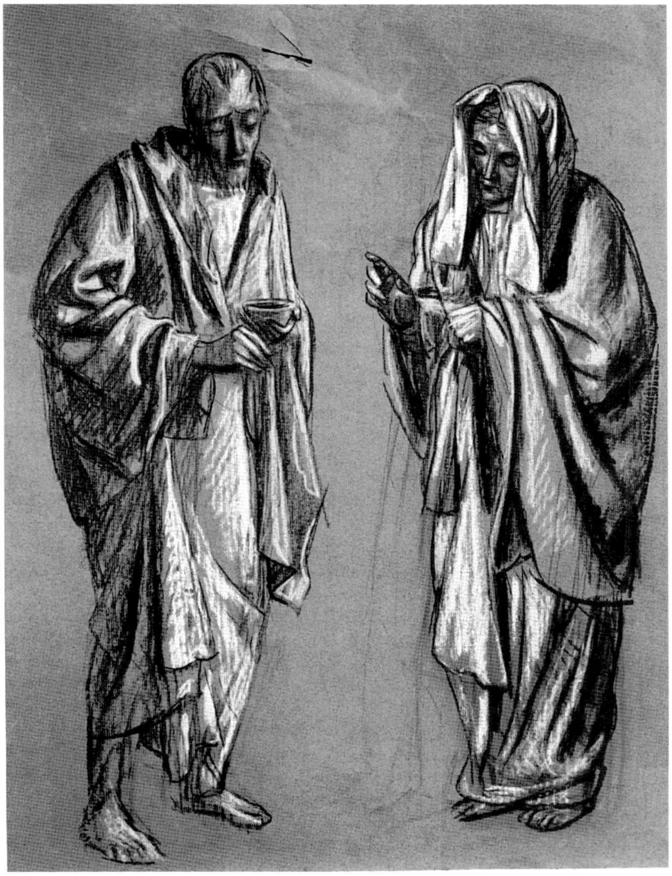

45

45 Studies for two figures for the *Crucifixion Triptych c.*1962 (M33)
Saint Ethelburga the Virgin within Bishopsgate, London EC2
Charcoal and pastel 630×490

46 Study for a group of three supplicating figures for *The Trinity in Glory* 1965 (M36)
Saint Alban the Martyr, Holborn, London EC1
Charcoal and white chalk 652×500
Signed *HF* and dated 14.6.65

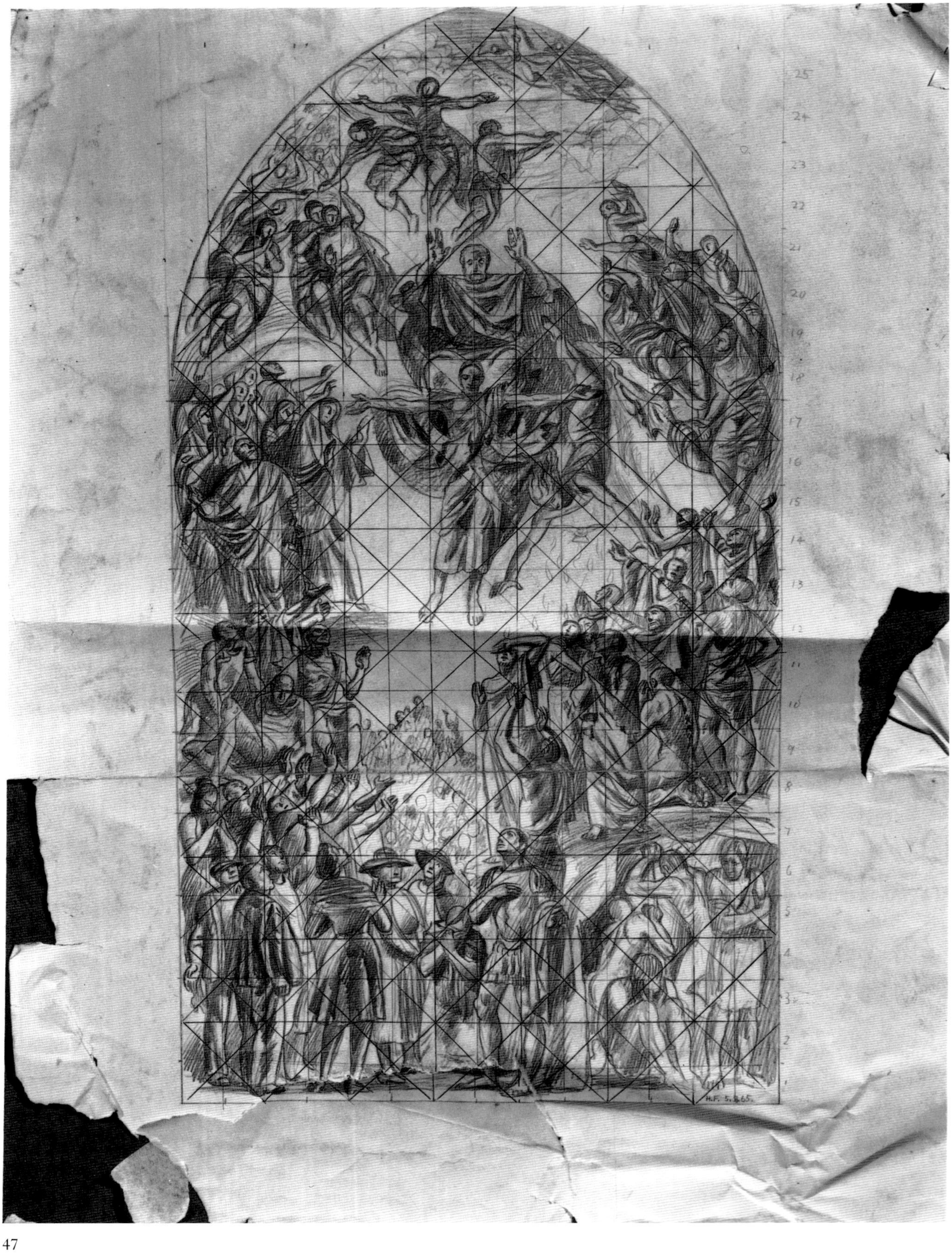

47

47 Gridded sketch for *The Trinity in Glory* 1965 (M36)
See Cat.46
Pencil and blue biro 755×560
Signed *HF* and dated 5.5.65

48 Sketch for *Stations of the Cross XIV: The Entombment* 1969 (M36)
See Cat.46
Gouache 545×750
Signed *HF* and dated

49 Sketch for *Stations of the Cross I: Christ before Pilate* 1969 (M36)
See Cat.46
Gouache 545×750
Signed *HF* and dated
Colour plate 6

50 Sketch for *Stations of the Cross V: Christ Carrying the Cross* 1969 (M36)
See Cat.46
Gouache 545×750
Signed *HF* and dated
Colour plate 7

51 Study of a mother and child for *The Madonna of the Sunflowers* 1984
Charcoal and pastel 640×320
Signed *HF* and dated
See colour plate 13 and Cat.62

52 Study of a pair of hands 1988
Charcoal and chalk 500×325
Signed *HF* and dated 8.11.88

53 Sketch for a mural of *The Ascension* 1992
Gouache 680×540
Signed *HF* and dated
Possibly intended for a church in Tewkesbury, but never executed
Colour plate 9

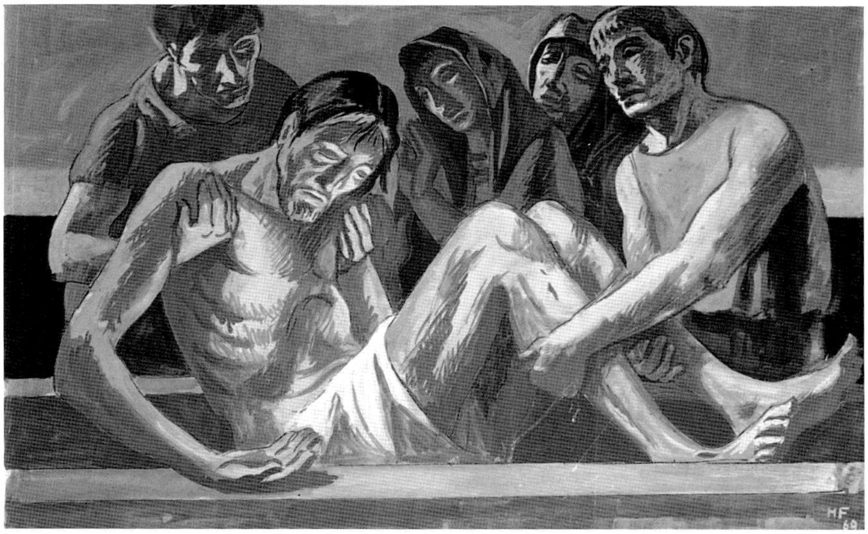

48

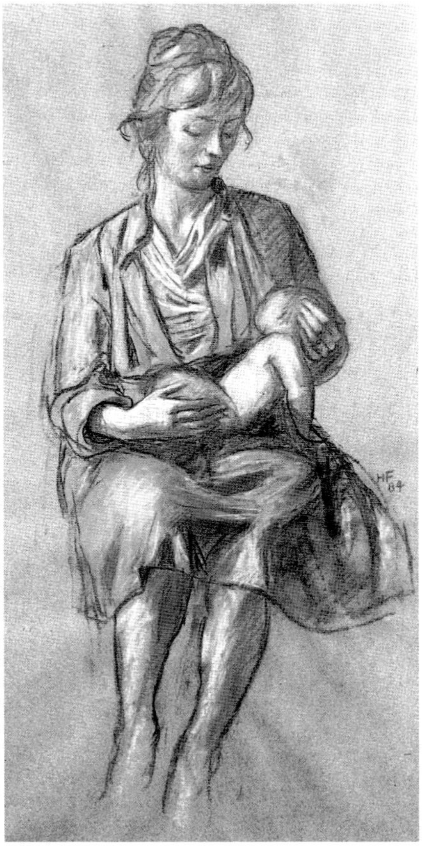

51

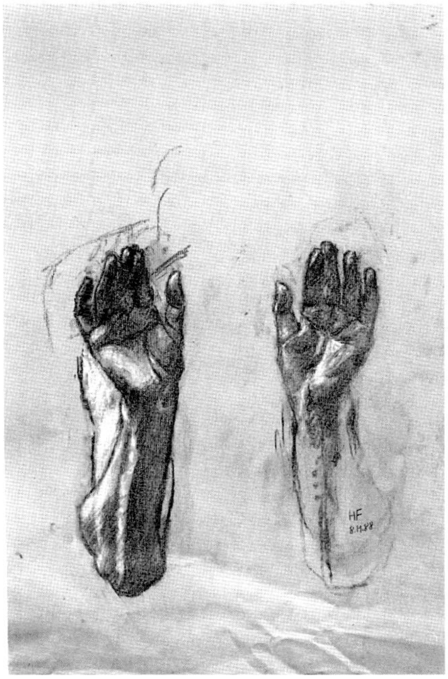

52

V Biblical and Mythological Paintings

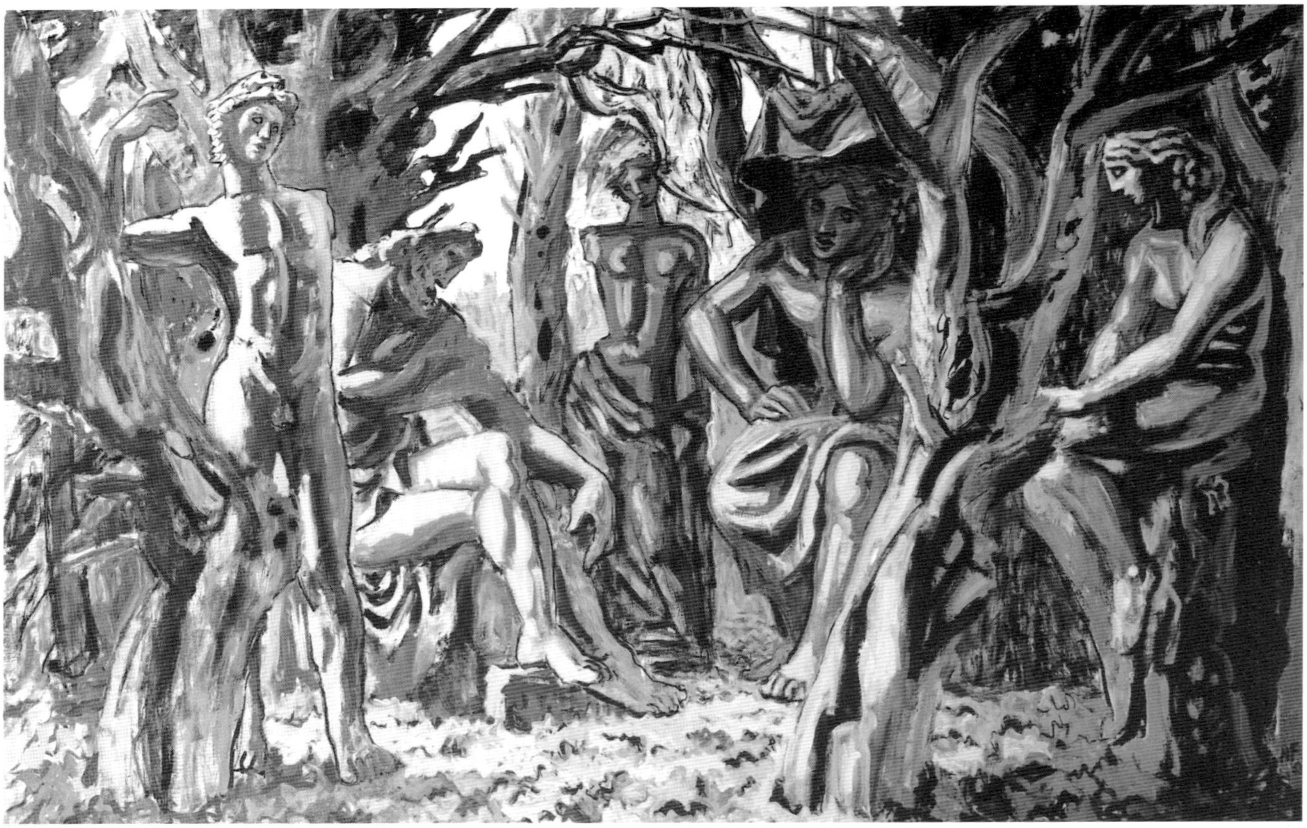

57

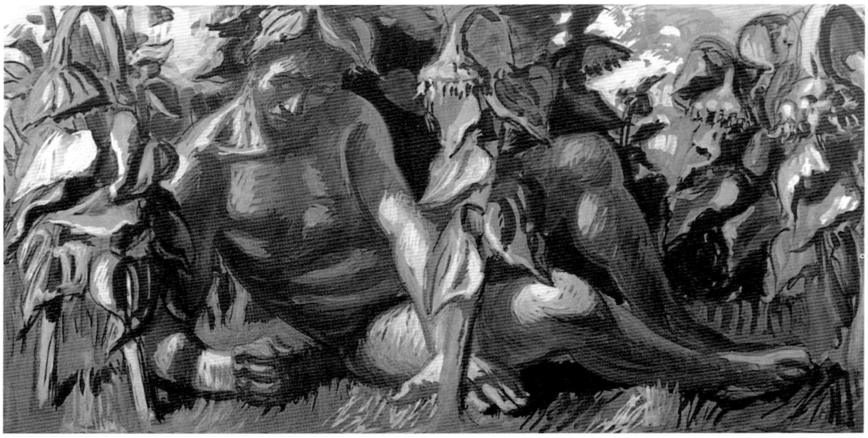

60

54 *The Prodigal Son* 1943
Oil on canvas 1525×660
Signed *HF* and dated
Colour plate 8

55 *Narcissus* 1946
Oil on canvas 606×915
Signed *HF* and dated
Colour plate 10; front cover illustration (detail)

56 *Lot and His Daughters* 1947
Oil on canvas 510×915
Signed *HF* and dated
Back cover illustration

With artists who can simply assume the attitude of Byzantine, Norman or Gothic style, I am not concerned here. They may even be truly religious; but theirs is an artistic insincerity which robs their work of the power to convince. To the others I would say: do not attempt to paint religious pictures unless you feel that you move naturally and gladly in the world out of which they come, and that you see there things which you can offer as your own contribution to the existing treasure of art. Bear in mind your responsibility towards the people who take your work in good faith and, although it is your own vision which makes your paintings valuable, do not let your personal idiosyncracies and temperament give them a distorted perspective.

Hans Feibusch, *Mural Painting*, 1946, pp.91–2

The Church has lost her superb taste and become used to the horrible, degraded things that commercial unscrupulousness has foisted on to her; of modern art she knows nothing. The artist is probably religious in his own way, but no longer conversant with the doctrine and ritual of the Church, and he has lost the conventions of religious art, the language in which former generations expressed themselves fluently. This language has more or less died during the interval, and our changed religious attitude makes the creation of a new one most difficult. Our innermost feelings may be as intense as of old, but we are shyer, less robust, more individually self-conscious, and less attached to traditional symbols. The creation of a new style of religious interpretation is made more difficult still by the fact that there exists no universal new style in art, but only a mass of personal impressions. So what are we to do?

Hans Feibusch, *Mural Painting*, 1946, p.90

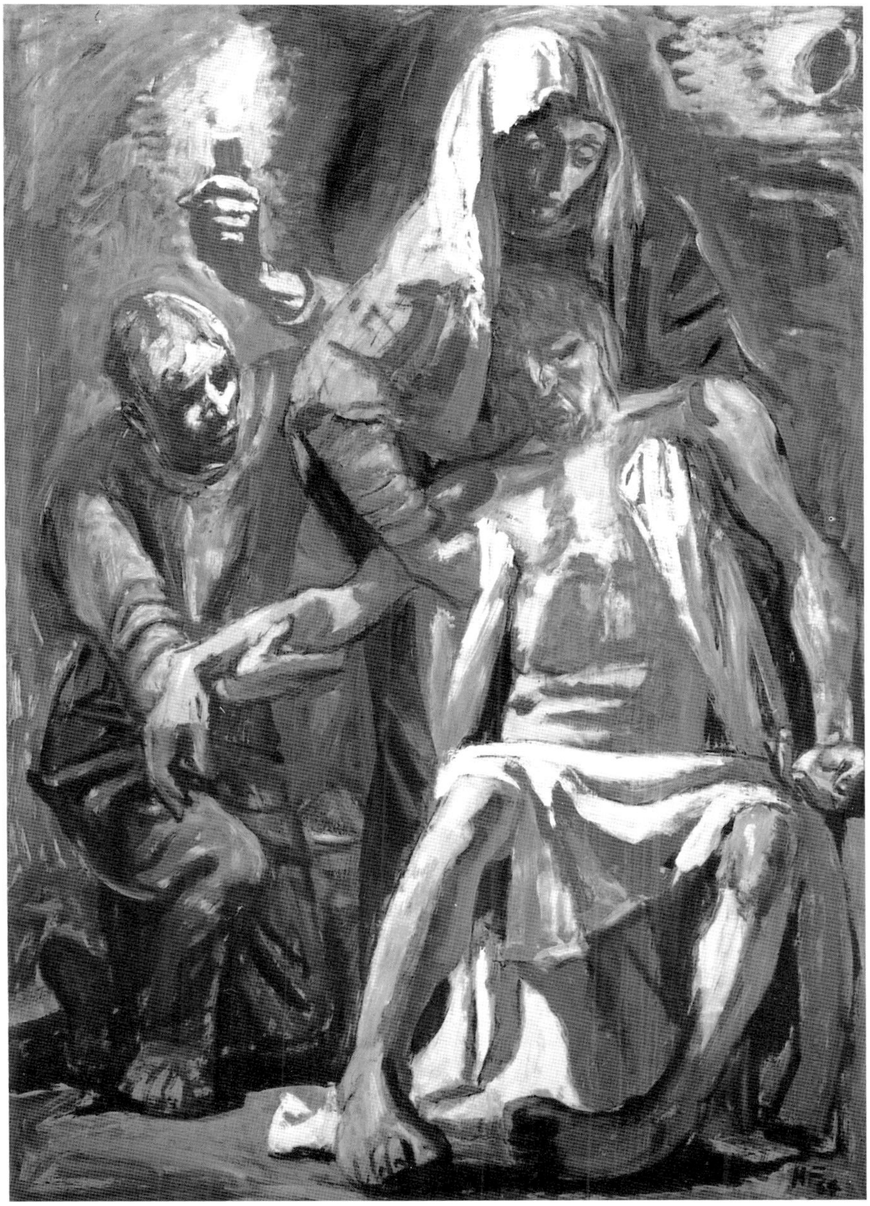

58

57 *The Old Gods* 1953
Oil on canvas 1528×2288
Signed *HF* and dated

58 *Pietà* 1964
Oil on board 1527×1073
Signed *HF* and dated

59 *The Four Seasons: Autumn* 1967
Gouache and watercolour 530×1035
Signed *HF* and dated
Colour plate 12

60 *The Four Seasons: Summer* 1968
Gouache and watercolour 530×1035

61 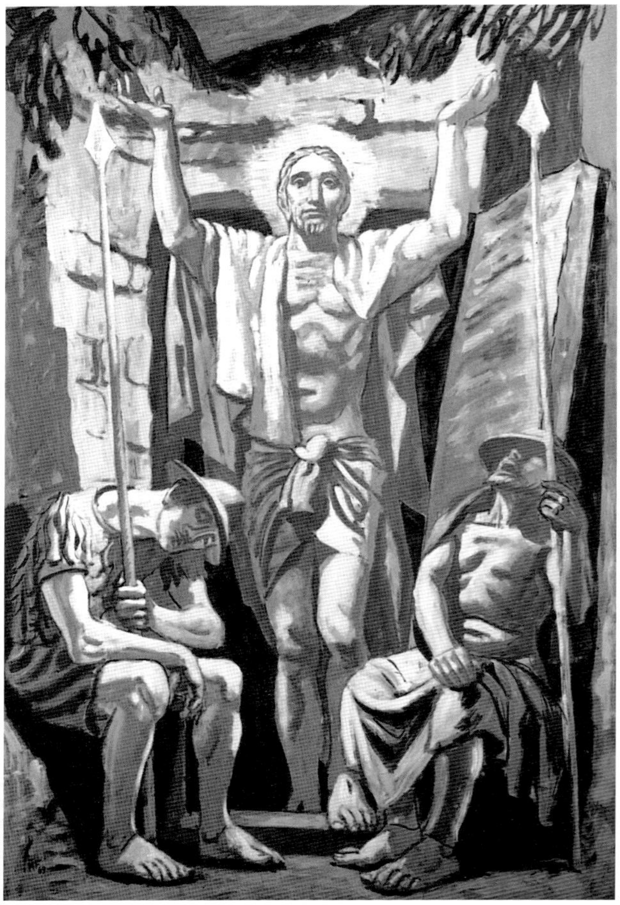

63 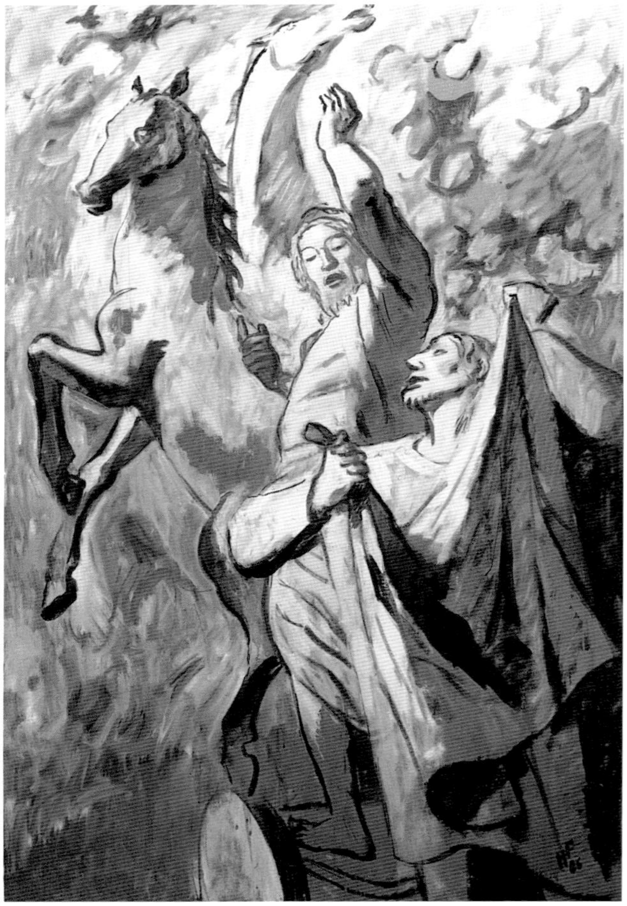

61 *The Resurrection* 1969
Oil on canvas 2286×1268
Signed *HF* and dated
Another version of this painting is in Christchurch, Saint Lawrence, Sydney, Australia

62 *The Madonna of the Sunflowers* 1984
Oil on canvas 1520×1065
Signed *HF* and dated
Exh: Royal Academy of Arts Summer Exhibition 1985
Colour plate 13; see Cat.51

63 *Elijah and Elisha* 1986
Oil on canvas 1777×1167
Signed *HF* and dated

64 *Crucifixion* 1986
Oil on canvas 1830×1370
Signed *HF* and dated

65 *The Footwashing* 1990
Oil on canvas 1100×1100
Signed *HF* and dated
Exh: *Images of Christ*, Northampton Museum and Art Gallery, 1993.
Illus: plate 11 in exh.cat.
Colour plate 11

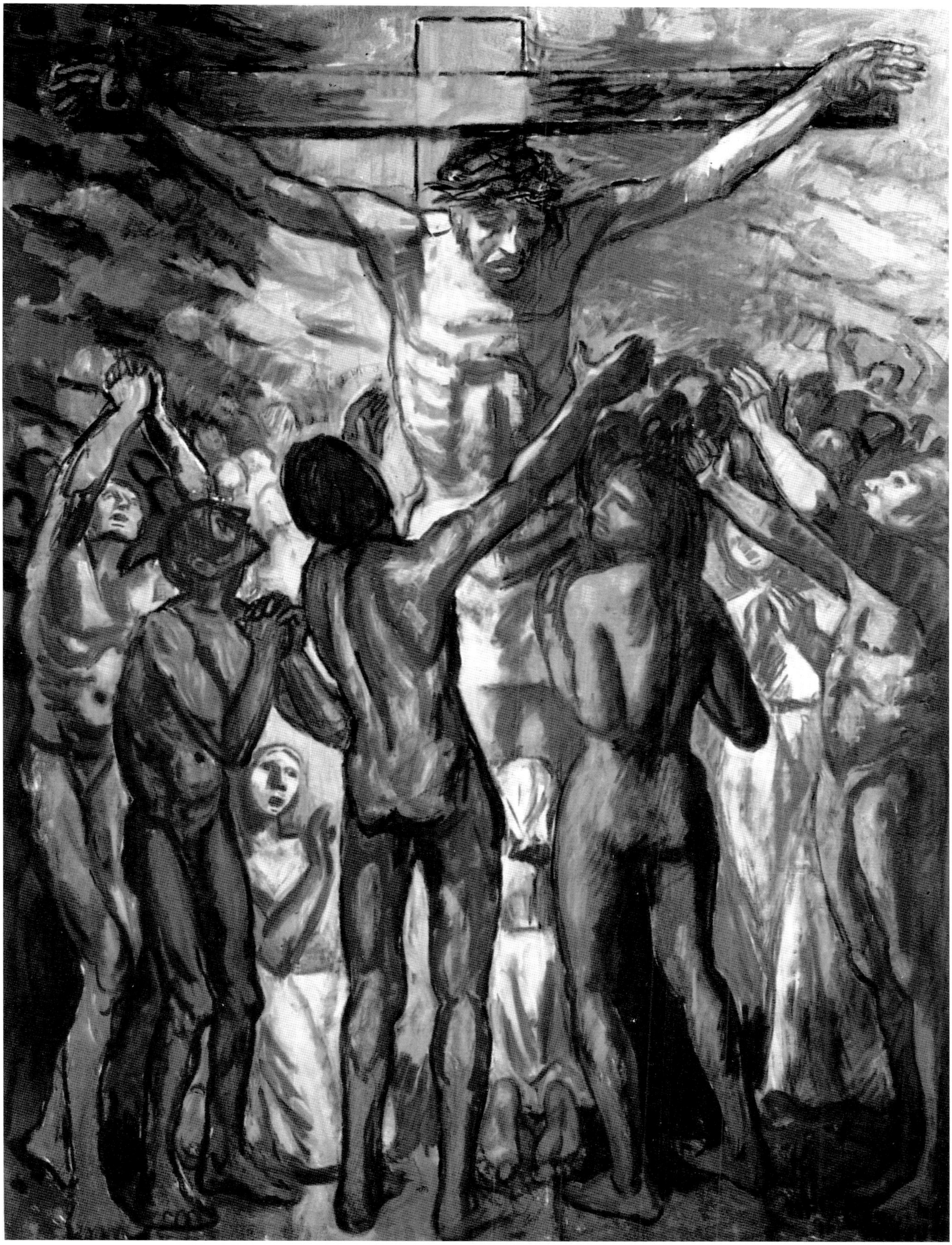

64

VI Landscape

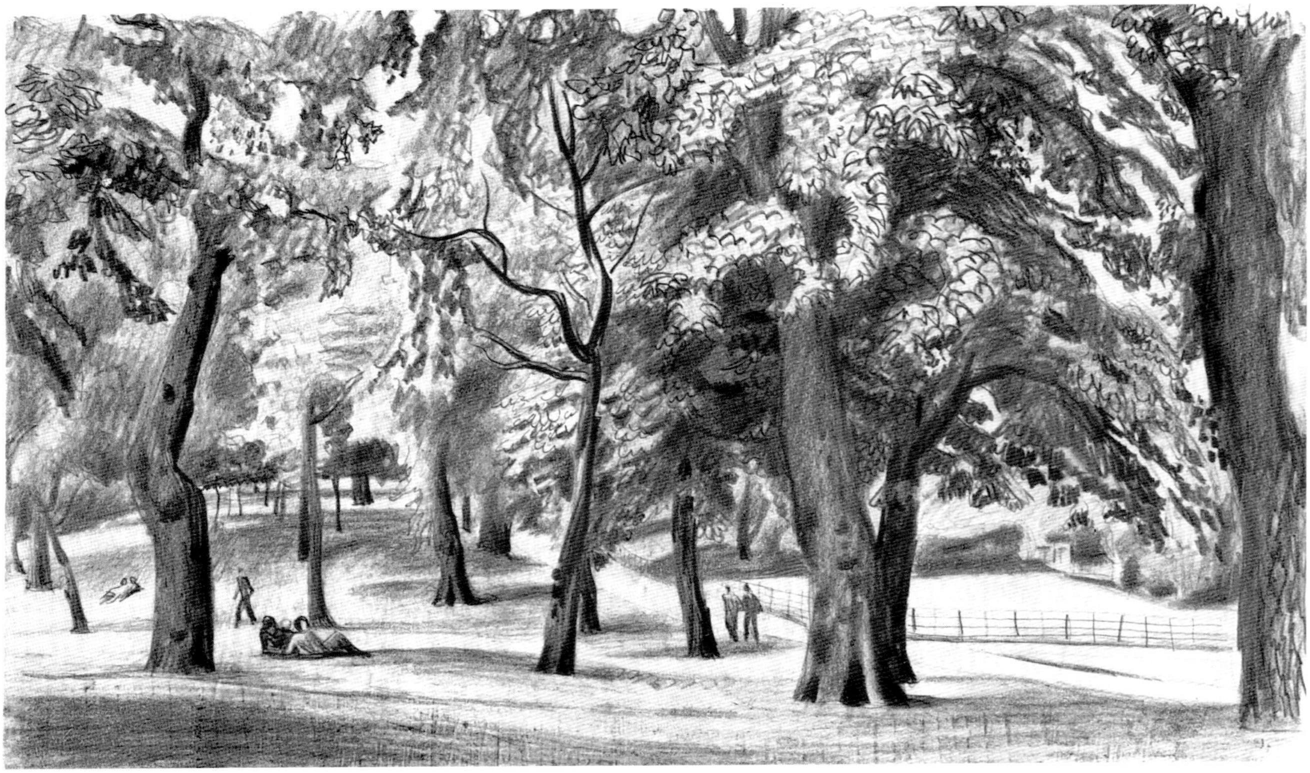

68

66 *Bomb Damage, London c.*1941
Pencil 230×355

67 *Bomb Damage near Saint Paul's, London c.*1941
Pencil 165×228

68 *Hyde Park, London* early 1940s
Pencil and chalk 220×355

Hans Feibusch was chiefly a landscape painter until his emigration. After his repeated visits to Italy, he produced a series of southern landscapes. In their clear and strong colours and the spaciousness and firmness of their composition they show the influence of his teachers. But the vitality of these expressive atmospheric landscapes imparts an intensity which is all Hans Feibusch's own.

From *Hans Feibusch*, 1979, Berlin, Galerie Michael Haas exh.cat. (Trans. Kathrine Talbot)

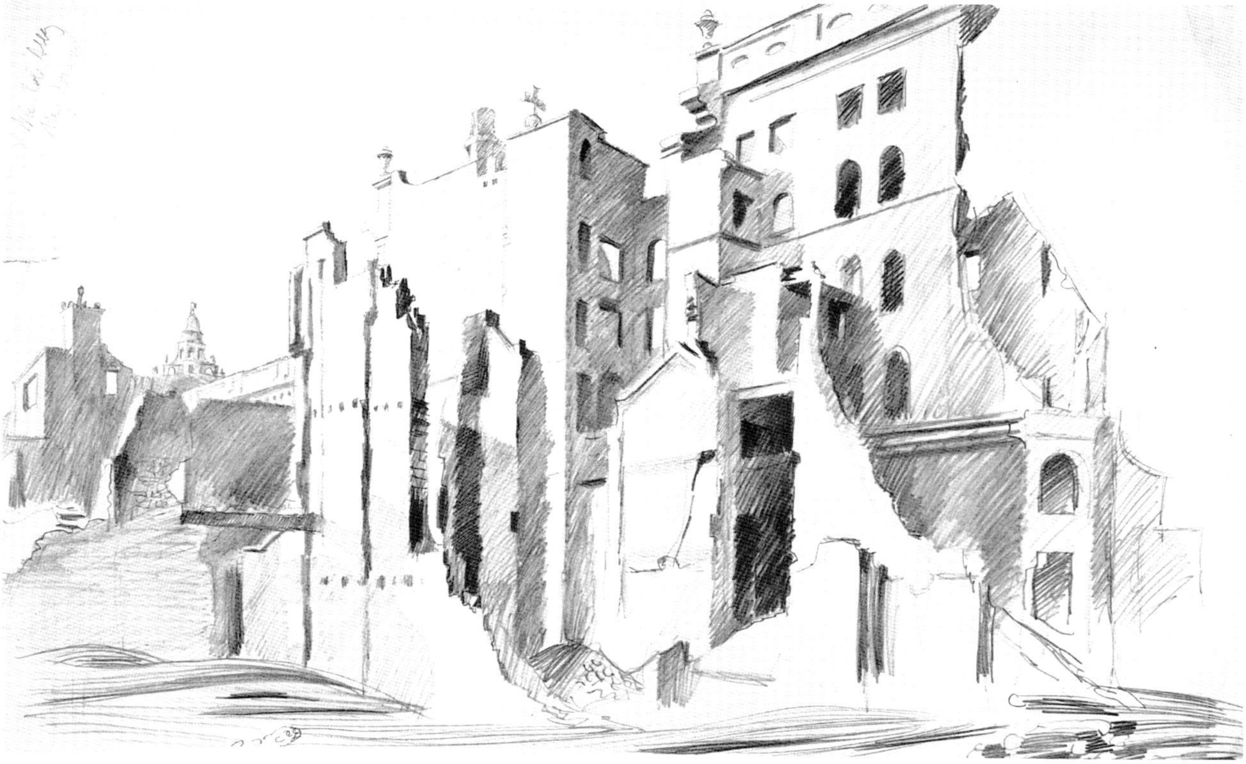

66

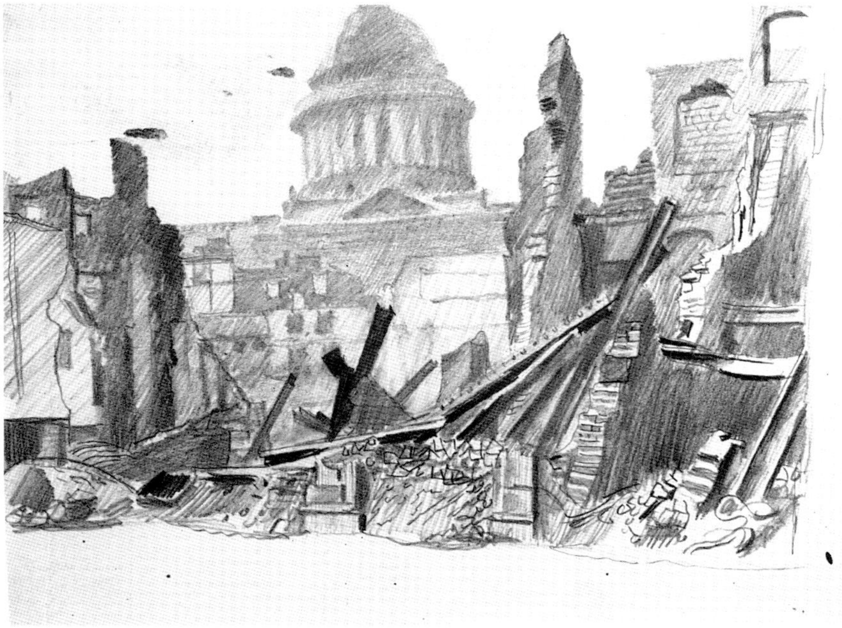

67

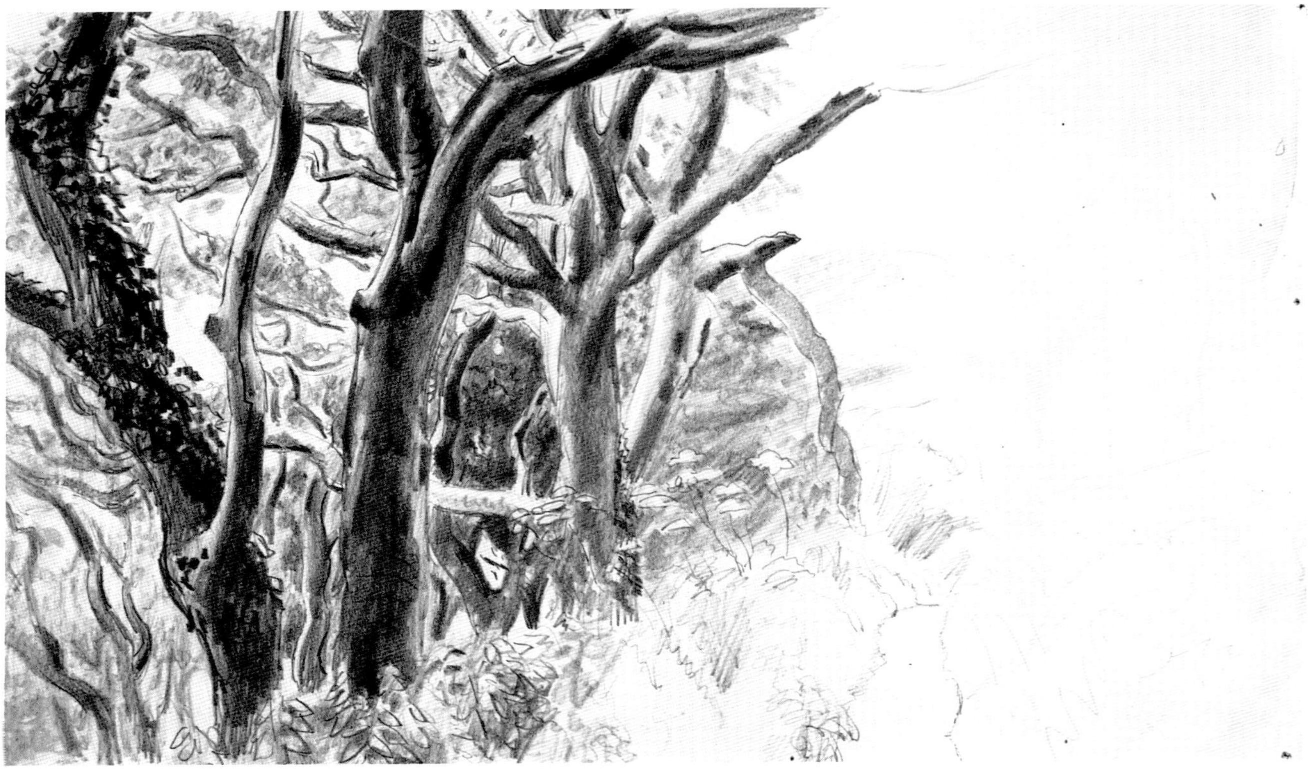

69

69 *Woodland Scene* (n.d.)
Pencil and chalk 213×355

70 *Study of Foliage* (n.d.)
Pencil and chalk 245×341

71 *Woodland Road* (n.d.)
Pencil 220×355

72 *Italian Landscape* (n.d.)
Pencil and chalk 268×348

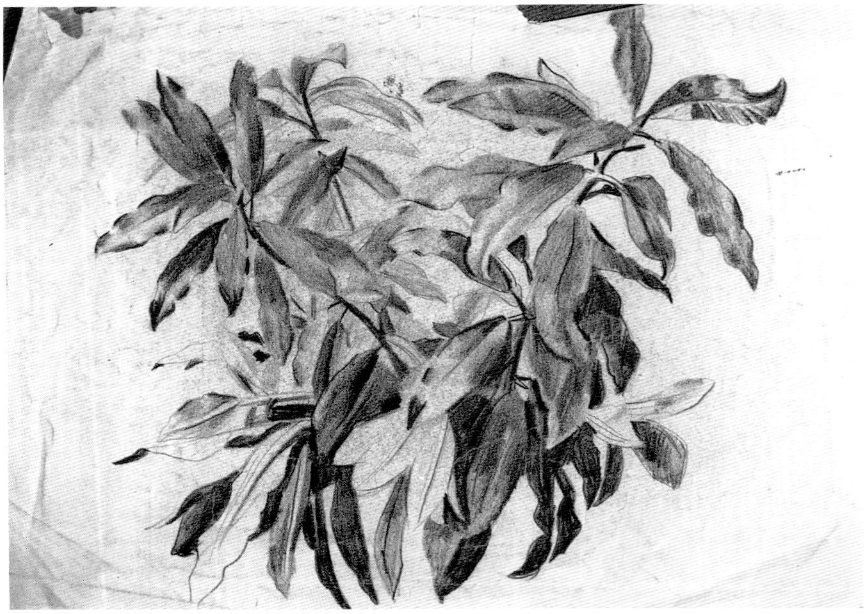

70

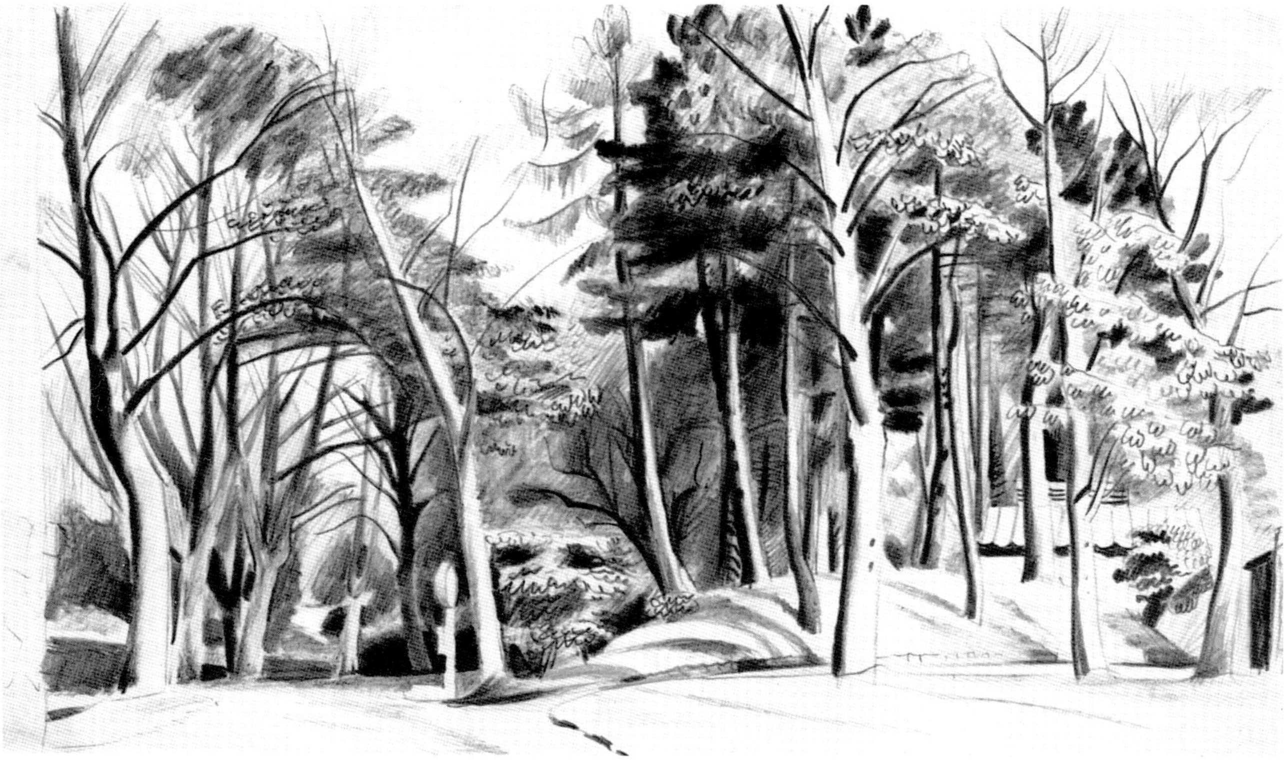

71

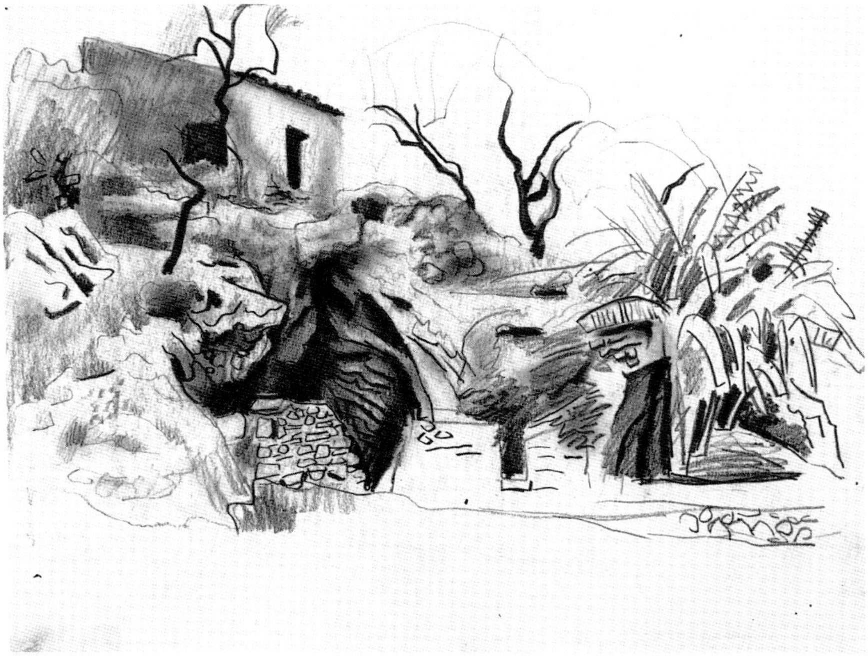

72

73 *Beached Fishing Boats, Sicily* 1949
Oil on canvas 500×920
Signed *HF* and dated

74 *The Bent Trees, Taormina* 1952
Oil on canvas 505×920
Exh: *Hans Feibusch: Ein Frankfurter Maler*, Historisches Museum, Frankfurt, 1986
Colour plate 14

75 *Dry Riverbed with Reeds* (n.d.)
Gouache 392×534

76 *Wye Valley Landscape* early 1960s
Gouache 380×540
Colour plate 15

77 *Yew Trees, Wye Valley* early 1960s
Gouache 430×530

78 *Brockweir - Artichokes and Poppies* early 1960s
Gouache 390×540
Brockweir was the house in Wales that Feibusch rented while he was working on the mural project for Newport Borough Council.

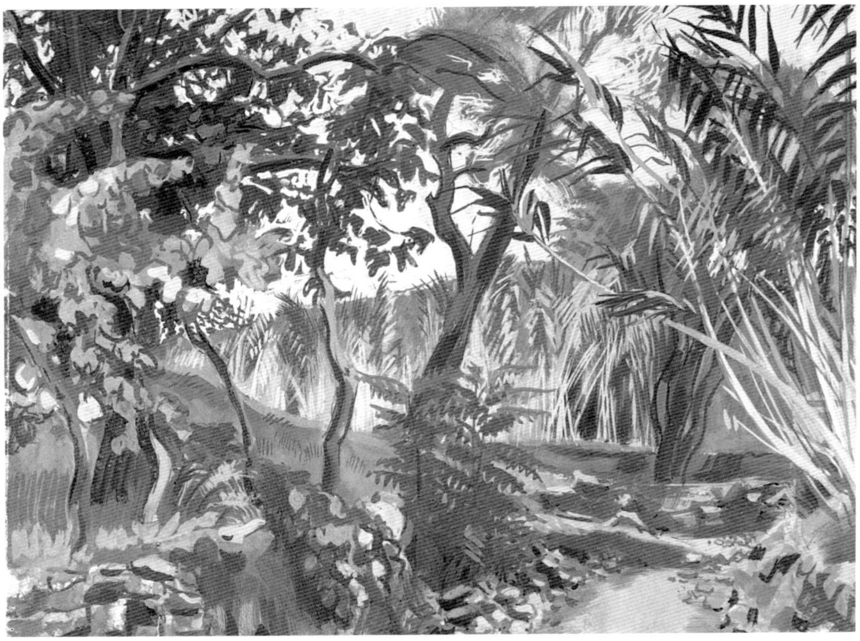

75

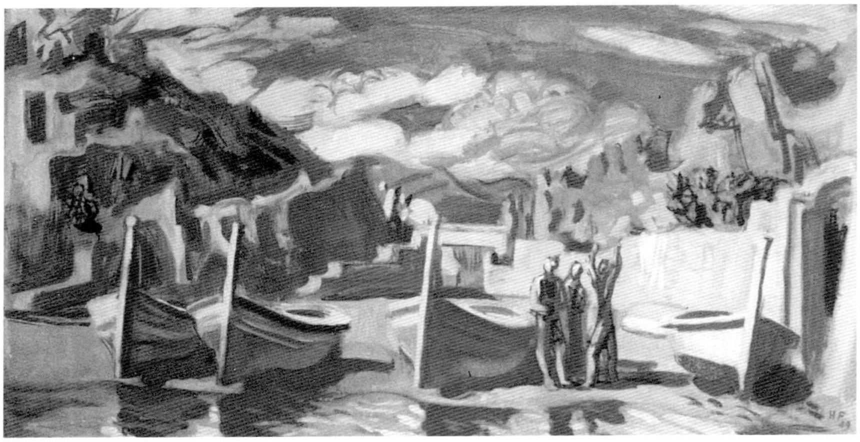

73

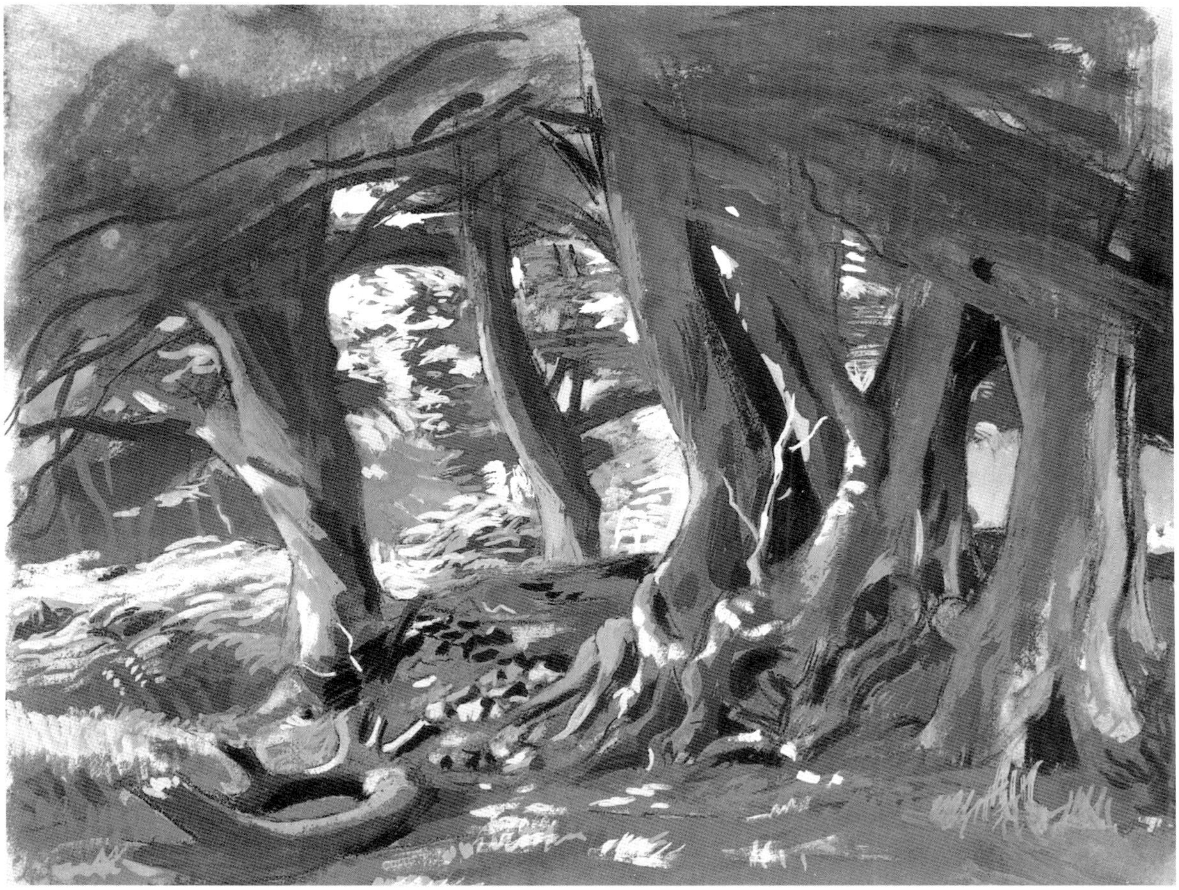

77

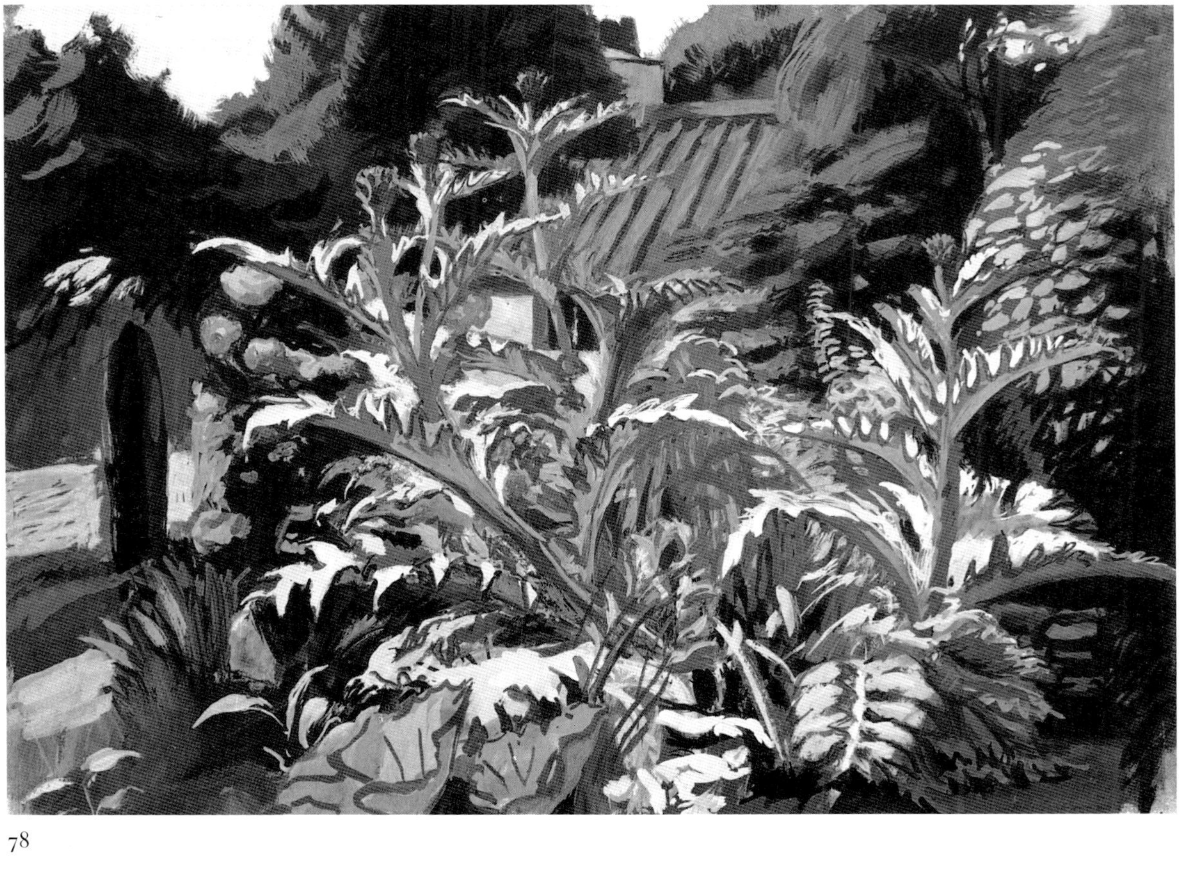

78

VII Sculpture

In the early 1970s, failing eyesight made Feibusch turn to modelling. Almost all the sculptures are modelled in clay and cast in resin, with a bronze patination.

79 *Portrait Head of Sir Clough Williams-Ellis* 1977
Cast resin h.394

80 *Europa and the Bull* 1978
Cast resin h.293

81 *Boy on a Hippocamp* c.1978
Cast resin h.285

82 *Palm Sunday* 1985
Cast resin h.450

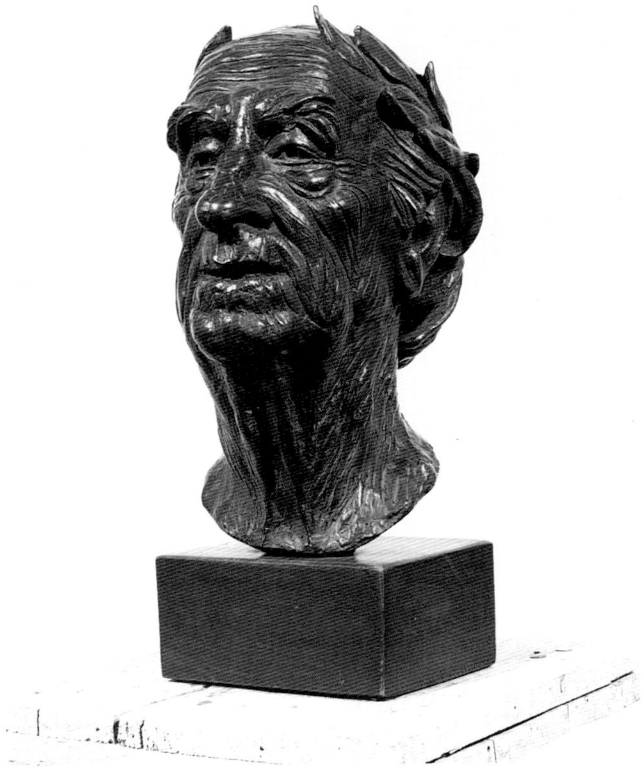

79

When I first took a lump of clay into my hands, I felt myself suddenly overcome by a passionate excitement towards this new world, that seemed to spring out of the depths of my being. Since then I have been modelling, my hands full of what my painter friend calls grey mud, trying to satisfy this craving for round forms. I battle with the stiffness of my old hands and the slowness of my old brain, the limitations of my sight and the tiredness of my old limbs, and when I look round the studio at the things I have made in those five years, I wonder whether I am not foolish to call myself a painter turned sculptor, instead of an old, worked-out painter playing with clay. Yet I love it; new ideas and shapes still rise in my mind, and I still hope to bring some of them to life.

Hans Feibusch in *Hans Feibusch: An Eightieth Birthday Exhibition*, Greater London Council exh.cat., 1978

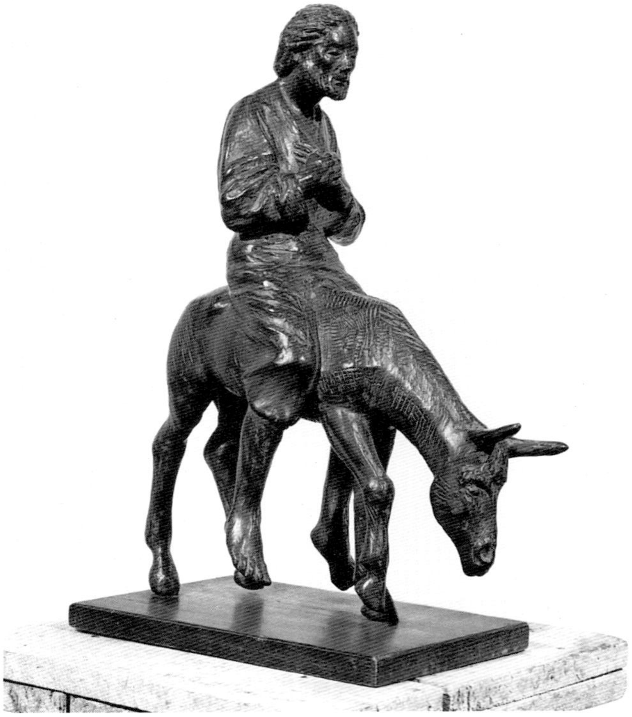

82

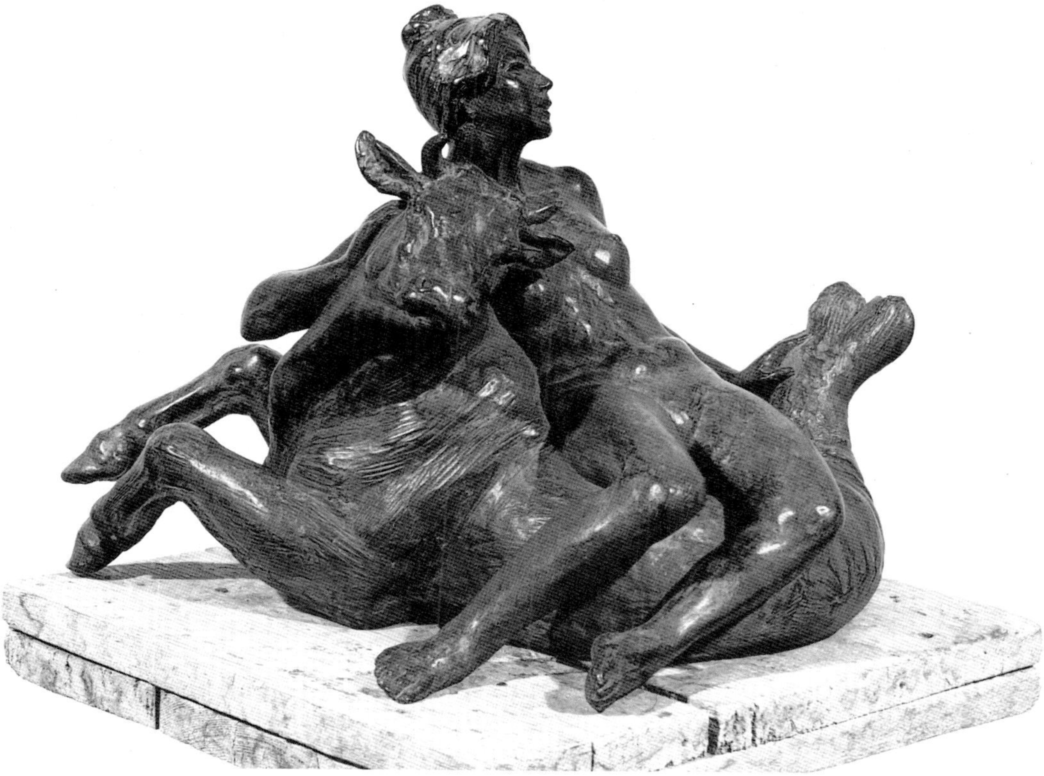

80

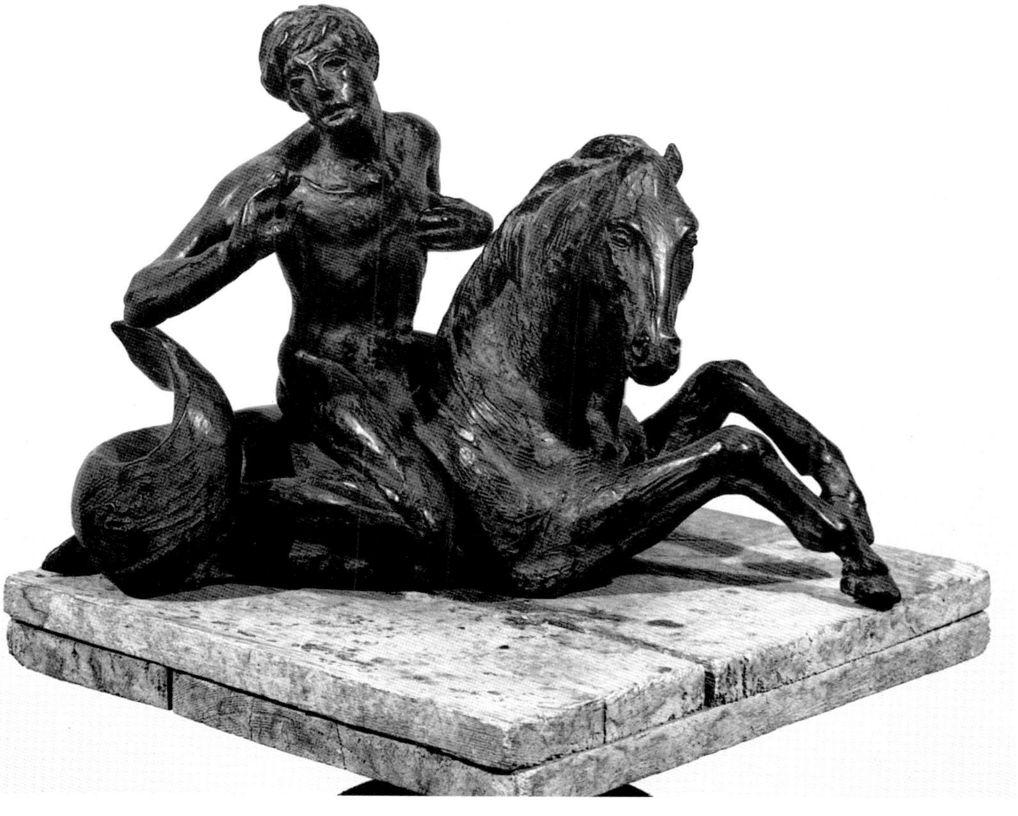

81

VIII Recent Work

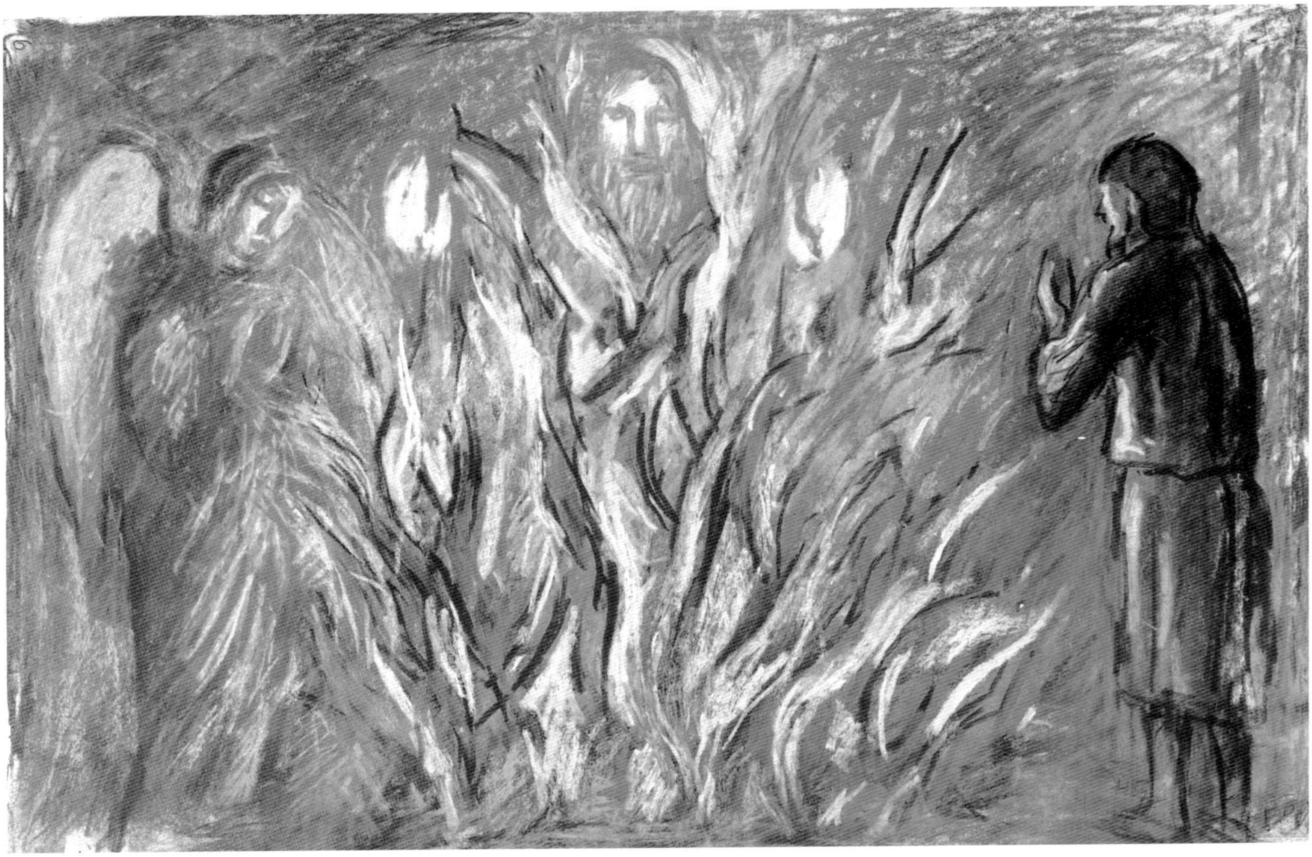

83

83 *Moses and the Burning Bush* c.1990
Charcoal and pastel 445×670
Signed *HF*

84 *Christ in the Wilderness* 1992
Pastel 630×490
Signed *HF* and dated

85 *Dream Subject* 1995
Pastel on card 772×566
Signed *HF* and dated
Colour plate 16

I have been using what strength I still have to paint a few more pastels, pursuing in them dreams which mostly go back to my youth, some to my earliest childhood, the very beginning of this century (when cognoscenti turned to Impressionism, while good Bourgeois from which I come still loved Böcklin and Feuerbach). Their romantic world has always lain hidden at the back of my mind and is now, when I have long since given up following the increasingly absurd jinx of today and been turning back to those childhood impressions, enforced by experience in life that took on a quasi-mystical weight, like the life in the deep forests of Russia during the 1st Great War.

The few works done during the last two years belong together in content and language, when the decrease of manual ability permits stronger, more direct expressiveness. It is an old age language of retrenchment and advance ...

Letter to David Coke of 20 January 1995

During a very long life the feeling of Divine impenetrability has gradually overcome all thoughts of Divine Justice in our sense. Fate (αναγκη) is what I see in life, and her often dark power ruling over us.

In the long hours I had to spend, as a soldier in the first war, alone in the huge black forests of Russia, their profound meaning impressed itself on me, and now, after many beliefs and changes over the years, comes slowly to life again, like so many meaningful pictures from long ago.

Letter to David Coke of 25 February 1995

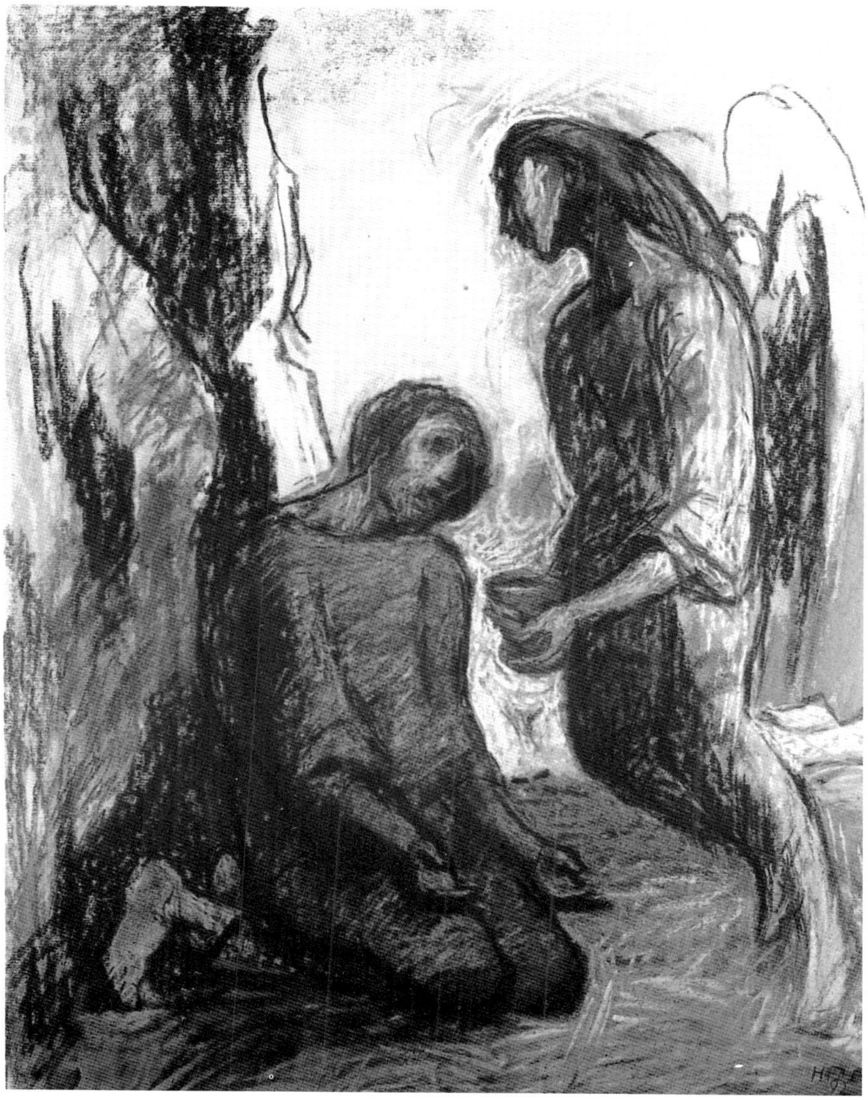

84

Bibliography

1 Writings by the Artist

1946
Mural Painting, London, A & C Black, 1946. With an Introduction by Sir Charles Reilly

'The Art of Mural Painting', published in six parts in *The Artist*, September 1946 – February 1947

1948
'Mural Painting', *Studio*, June 1948

1950
Foreword to *Society of Mural Painters: First Exhibition*, London, Arts Council of Great Britain exh.cat., 1950

1954
'Mural Paintings in Churches', *Theology*, no.403, Vol. LVII, January 1954, pp.3–8

'Mural Paintings in Churches', *Studio*, April 1954, p.106

1978
'Hans Feibusch writes …', in *Hans Feibusch: An Eightieth Birthday Exhibition*, London, Greater London Council exh.cat., 1978.

1986
'Mein Leben', in Rita Rücker (ed.), *Hans Feibusch: Ein Frankfurter Maler*, Frankfurt, Historisches Museum exh.cat., 1986

(Feibusch gave an archive of papers to the Stadtarchiv in Frankfurt in 1961. No.S2/1540)

2 Books Illustrated by the Artist

1946
The Revelation of Saint John the Divine, London, Collins, 1946. With thirteen original lithographs and endpapers by Feibusch

3 Exhibition Catalogues

1934
Paintings by Hans Feibusch, London, Lefevre Gallery exh.cat., 1934. With an Introduction by James Laver

1942
Religious and Other Paintings by Hans Feibusch, London, Lefevre Gallery exh.cat., 1942

1978
Hans Feibusch and James L. Kennedy, *Hans Feibusch: An Eightieth Birthday Exhibition*, London, Greater London Council exh.cat., 1978

1979
Hans Feibusch, Berlin, Galerie Michael Haas exh.cat., 1979

1986
Rita Rücker (ed.), *Hans Feibusch: Ein Frankfurter Maler*, Frankfurt, Historisches Museum exh.cat., 1986. With texts by Bishop Peter Walker, Hans Feibusch, Rita Rücker and Pamela Wedgwood

4 English Periodical and Newspaper Articles

1934
E. Maxwell Fry, 'Hans Feibusch', *Architectural Review* 75, June 1934, pp.215–16. Review of the 1934 one-man exhibition at the Lefevre Gallery, London

London Commentary section, *Studio*, February 1934, p.62. Review of the 1934 one-man exhibition at the Lefevre Gallery, London

1946
Studio, December 1946, p.191. Review of Feibusch's lithographs for *The Revelation of Saint John the Divine*

1947
Barbara Jones, *Architectural Review* 101, March 1947, p.111. Review of *Mural Painting*

Herbert Read, *Burlington Magazine* 537, Vol. LXXXI, December 1947, p.357. Review of *Mural Painting*

1949
Eric Newton, 'Hans Feibusch: Mural Painter', *Studio*, March 1949, pp.74–9. (Reproduced in this catalogue on p.17)

1957
Elfrieda Vipont, *The High Way*, Oxford, Oxford University Press, 1957. Illustration of *Footwashing* (1938) in Colliers Wood

1985
Tom Devonshire-Jones, 'A Modern Master: The Impact on Church Art of Hans Feibusch', *Church Building*, Whitsun 1985, pp.16–18

1993
John Russell Taylor, 'A Life that Spans the Century', *The Times*, 11 August 1993